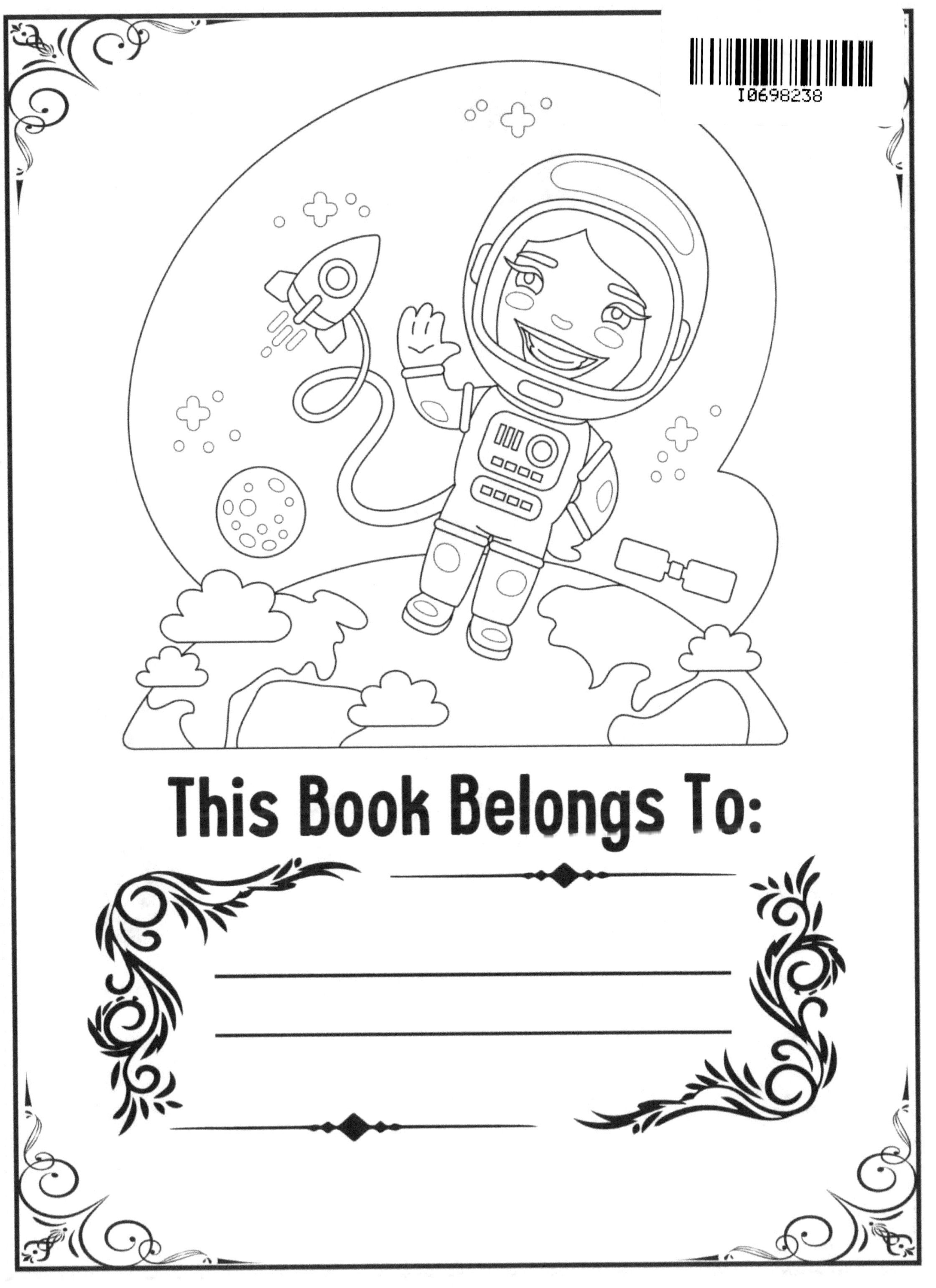

This Book Belongs To:

COLOR TEST

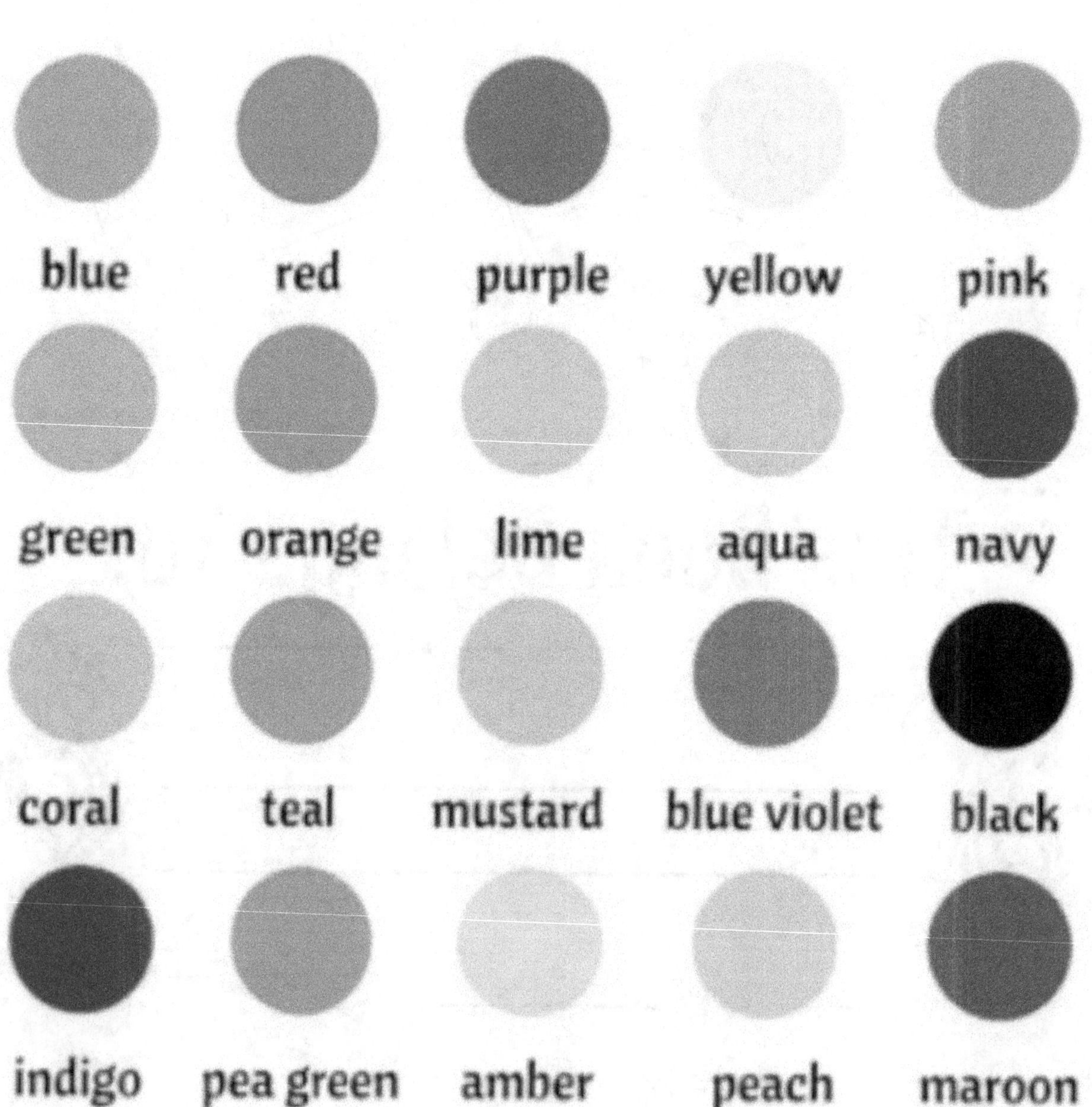

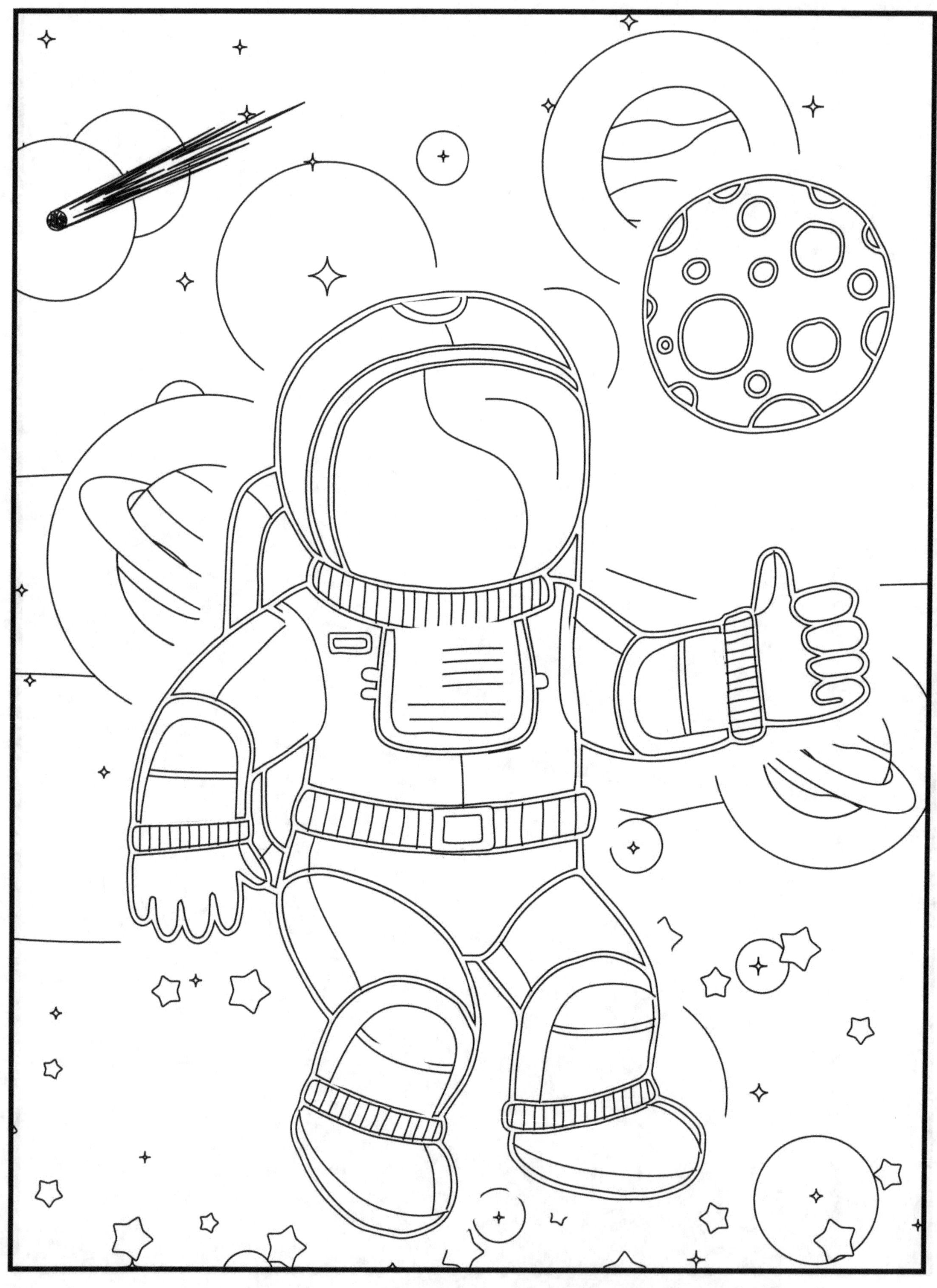

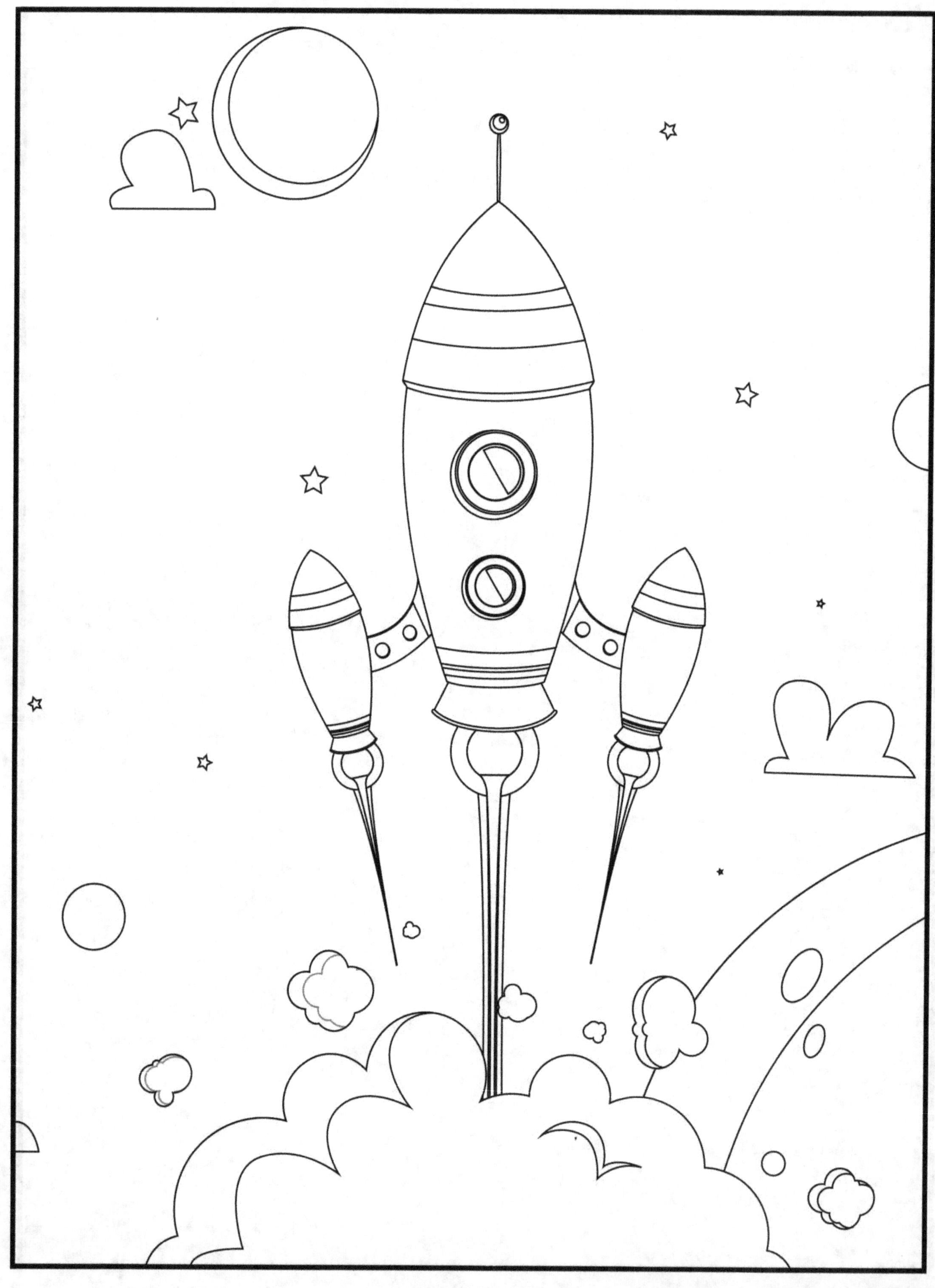

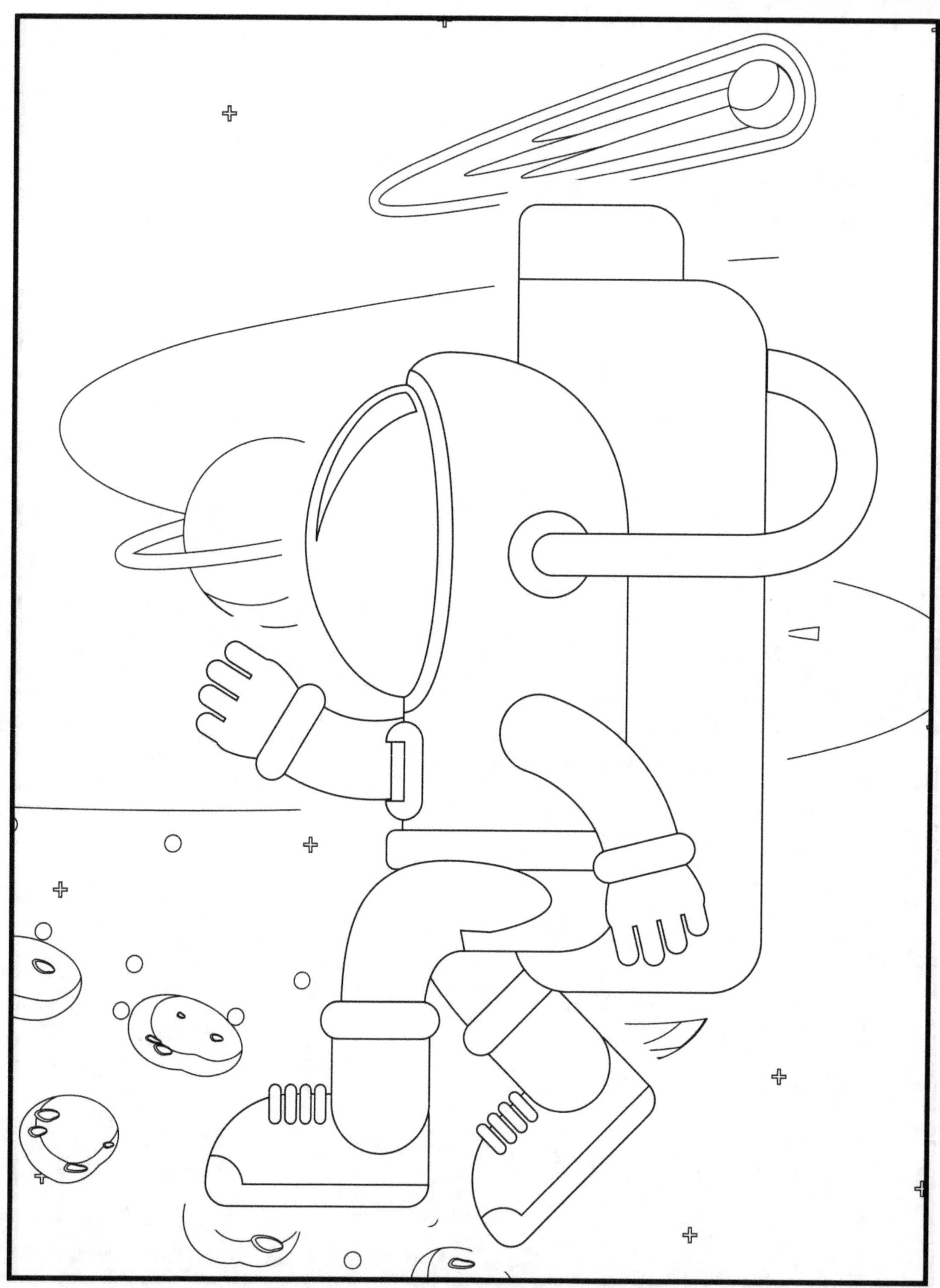

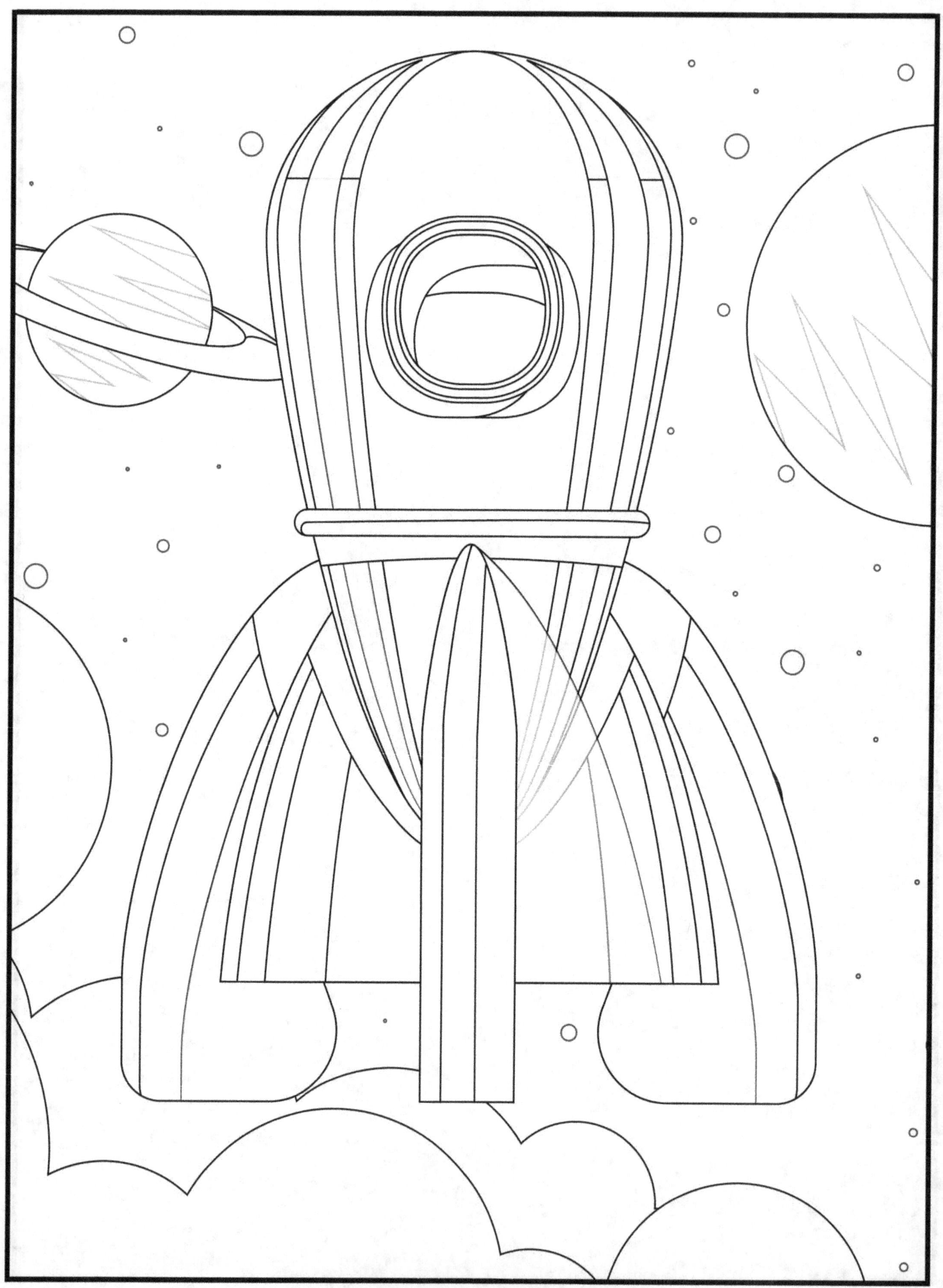

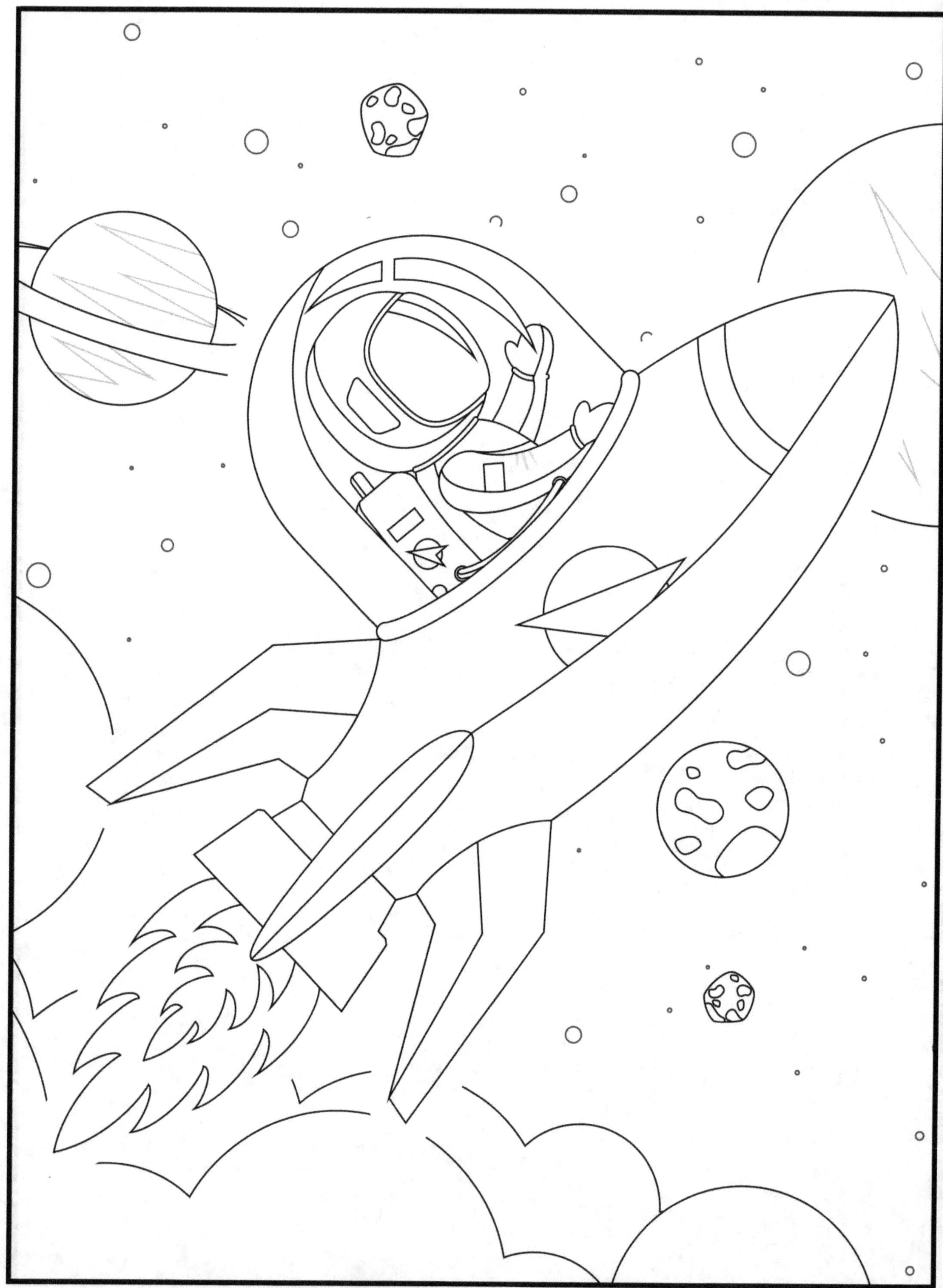

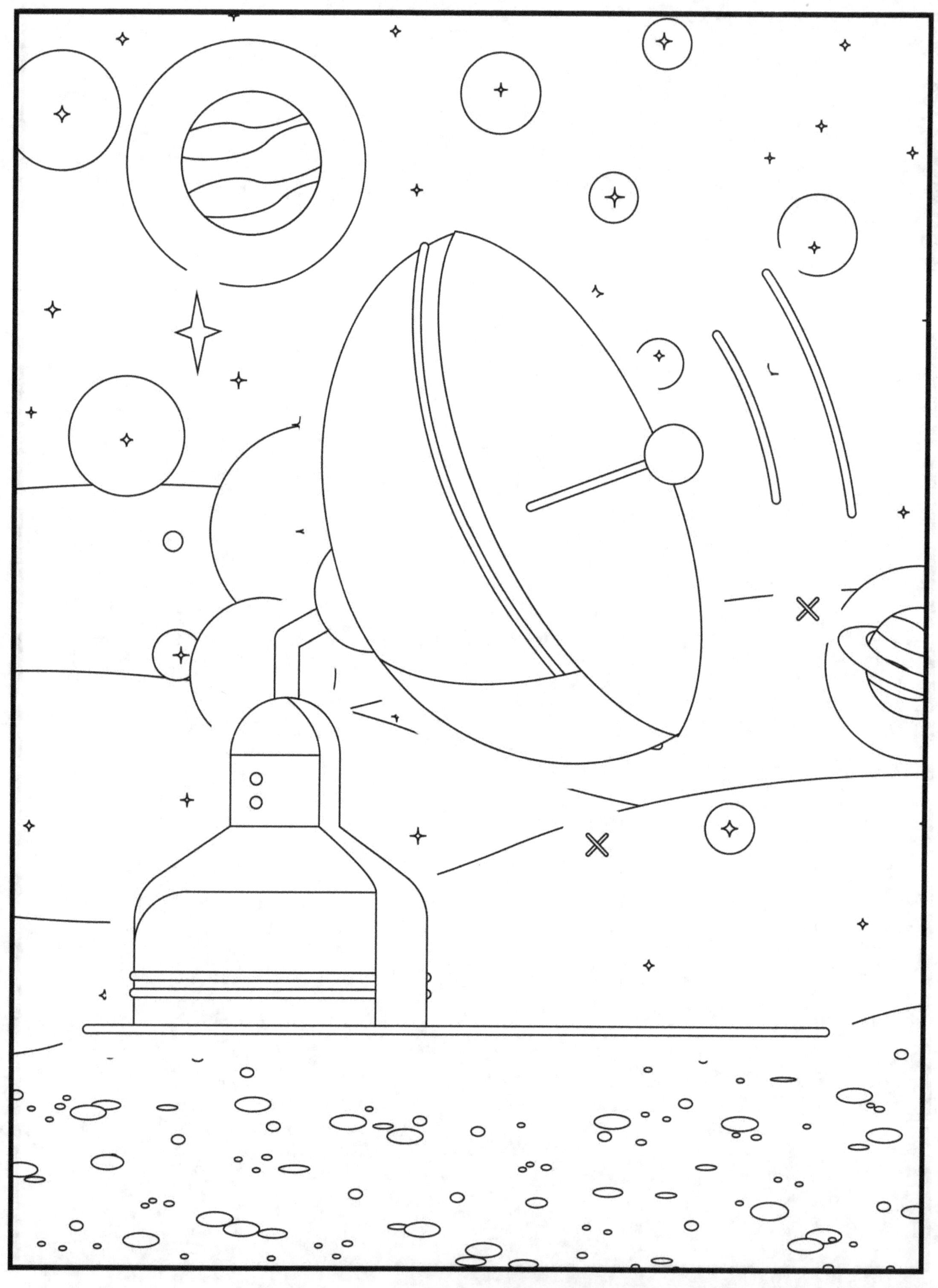

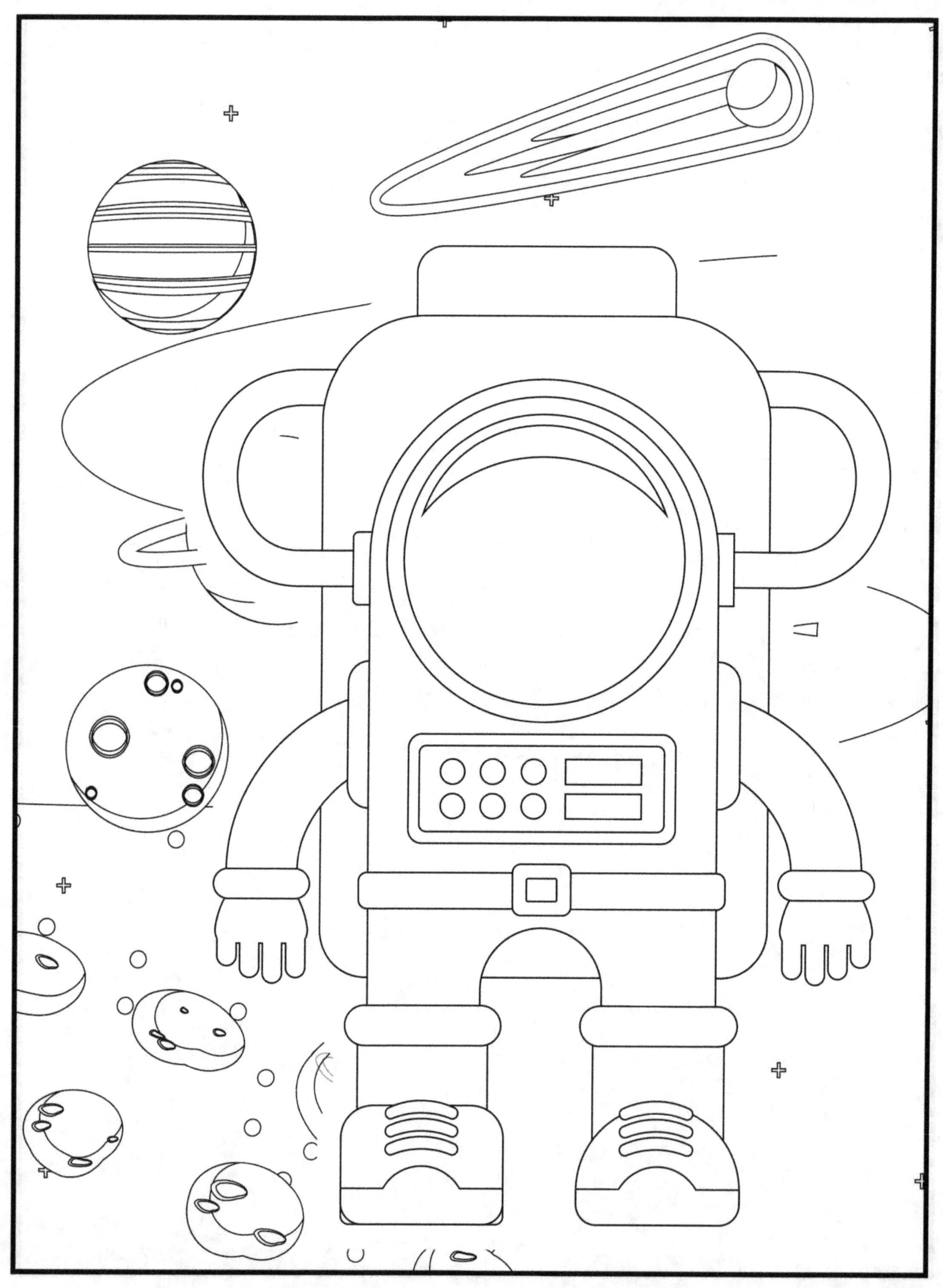

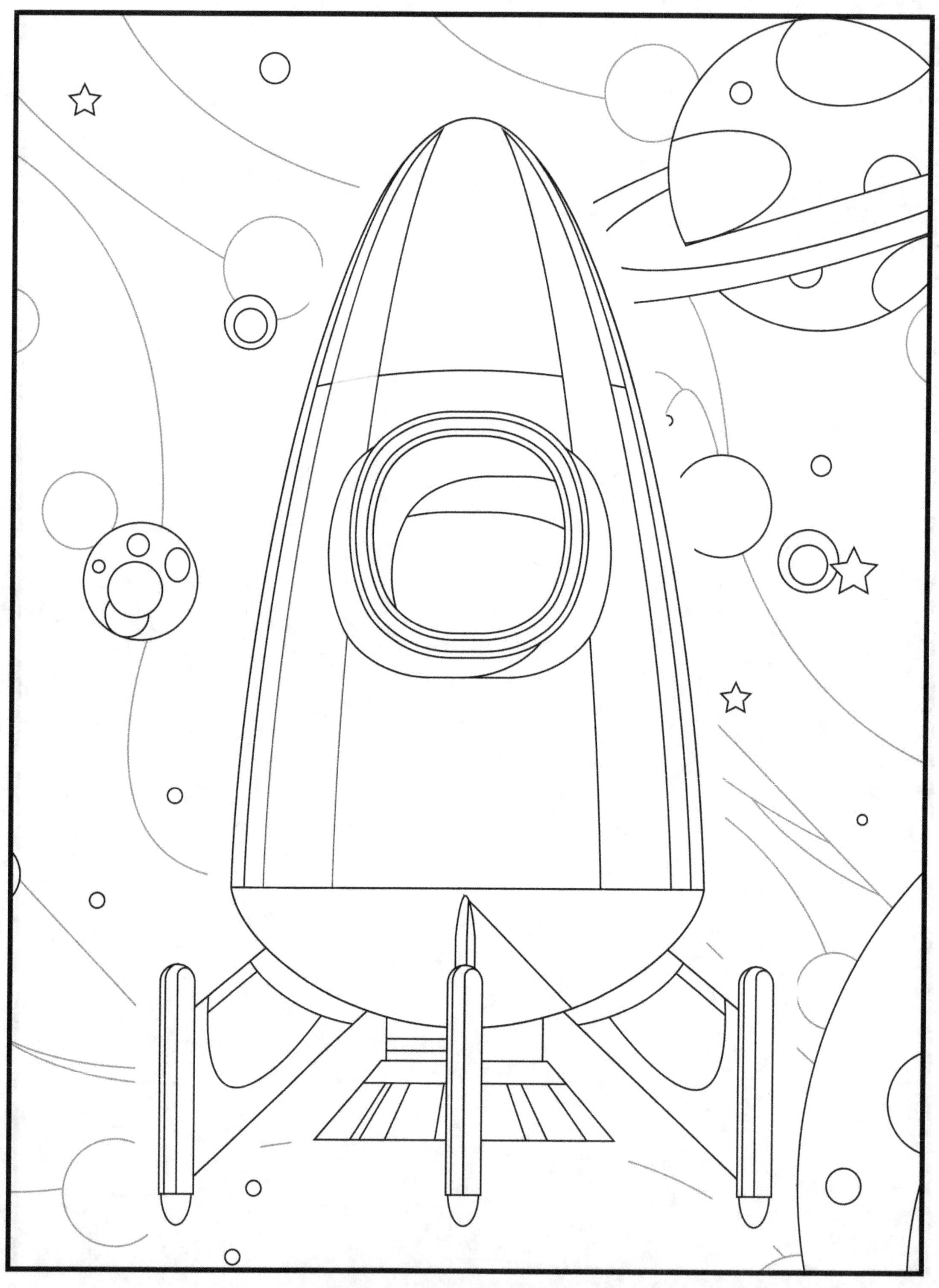

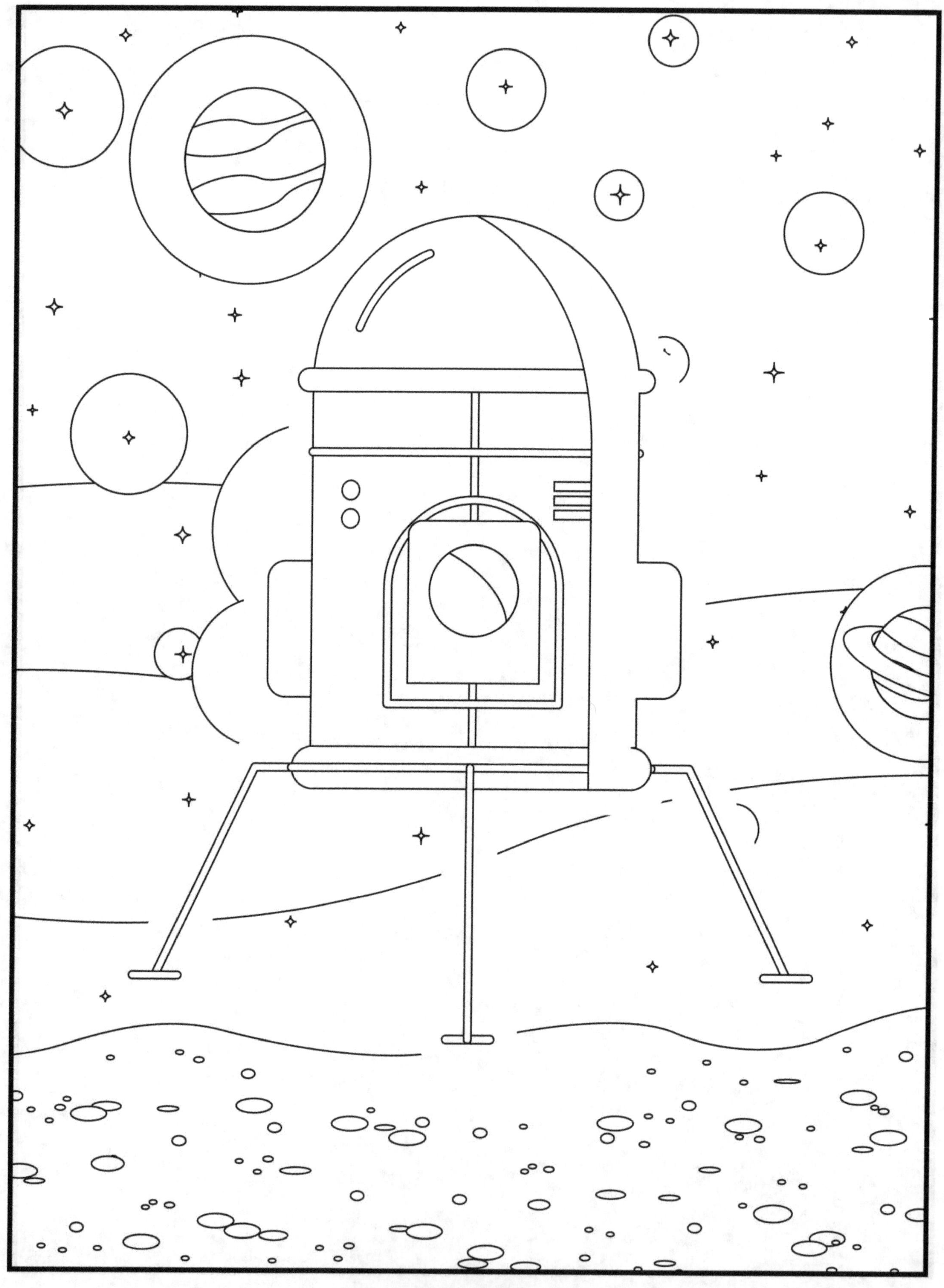

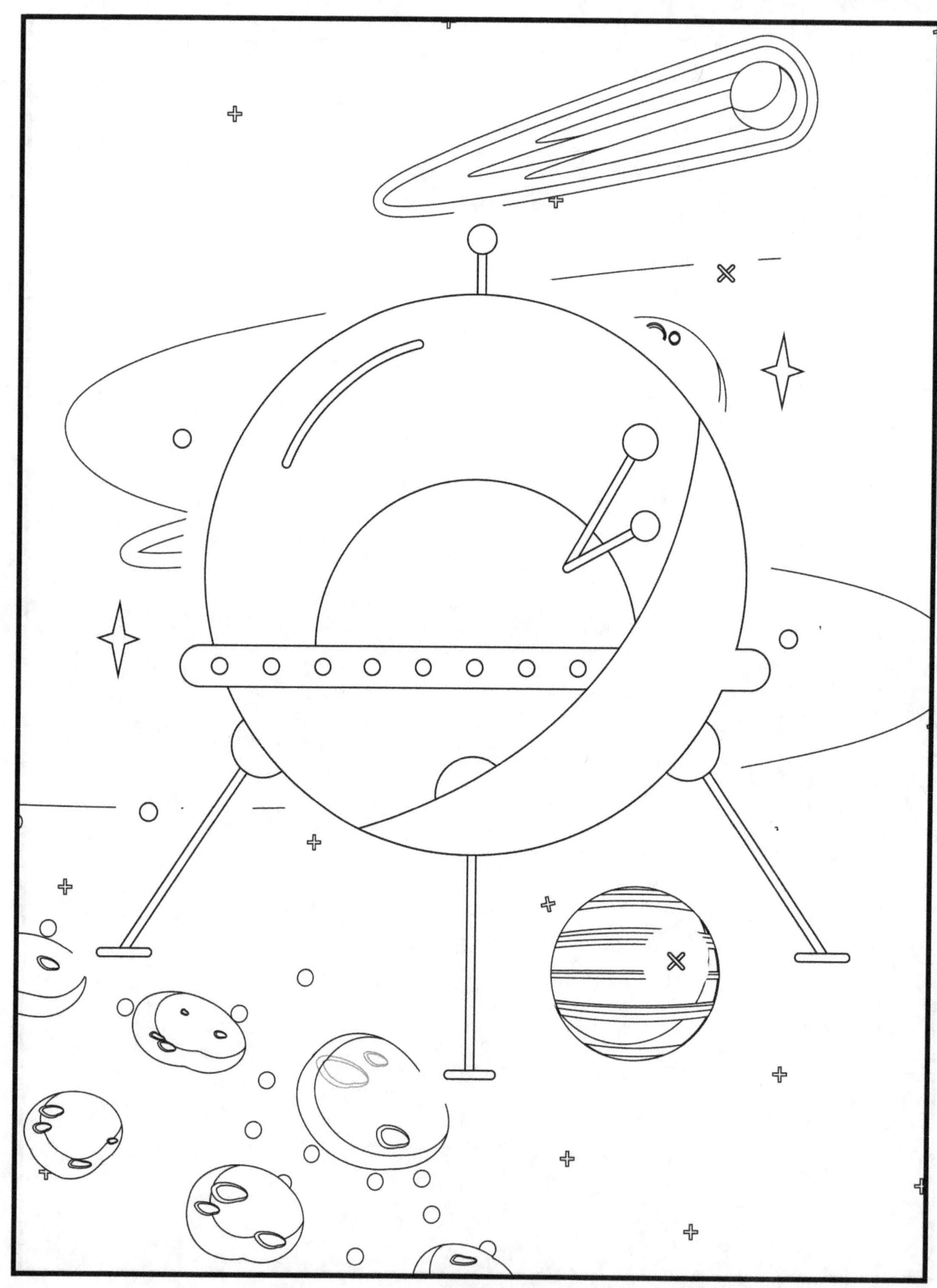

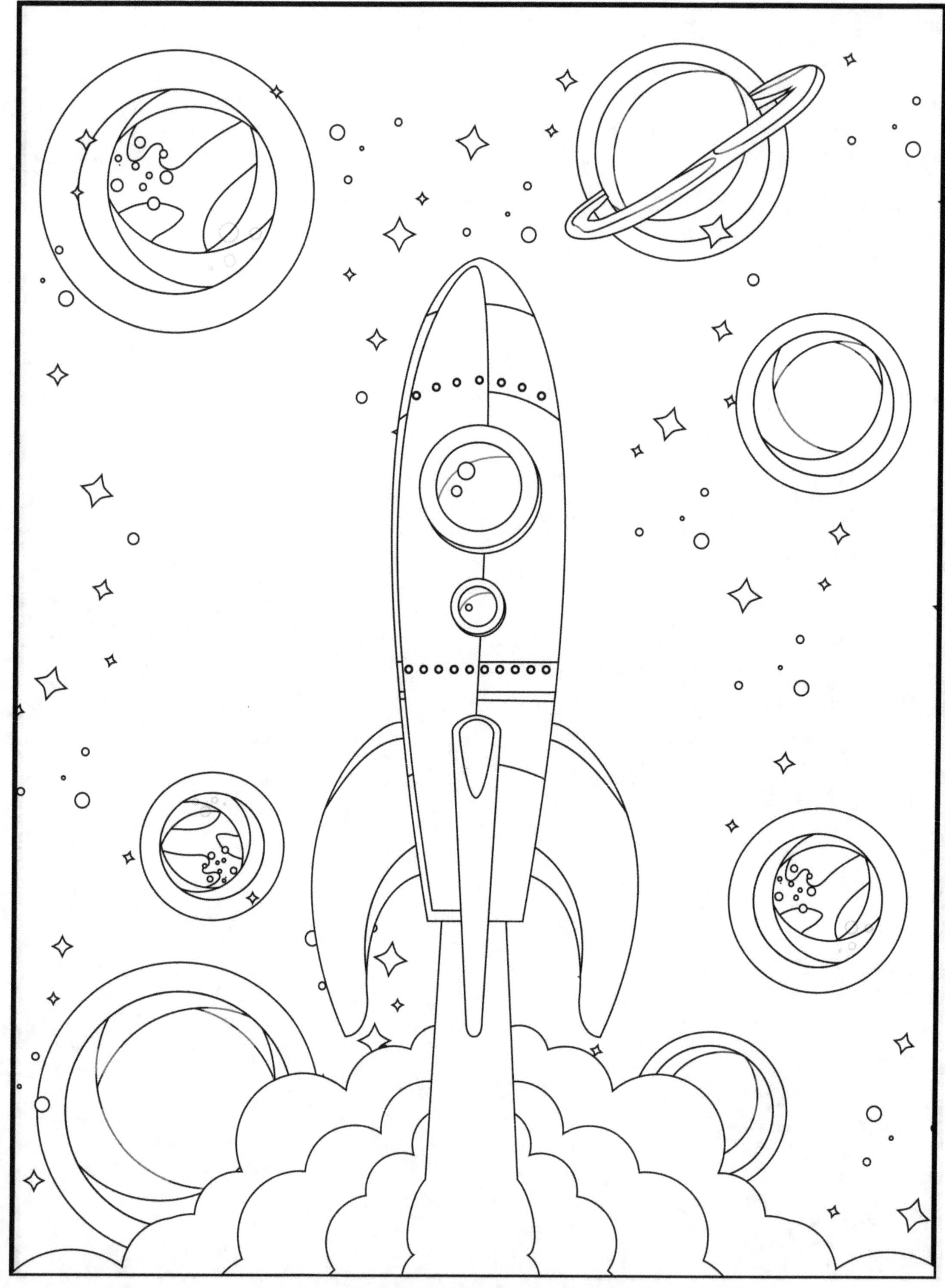

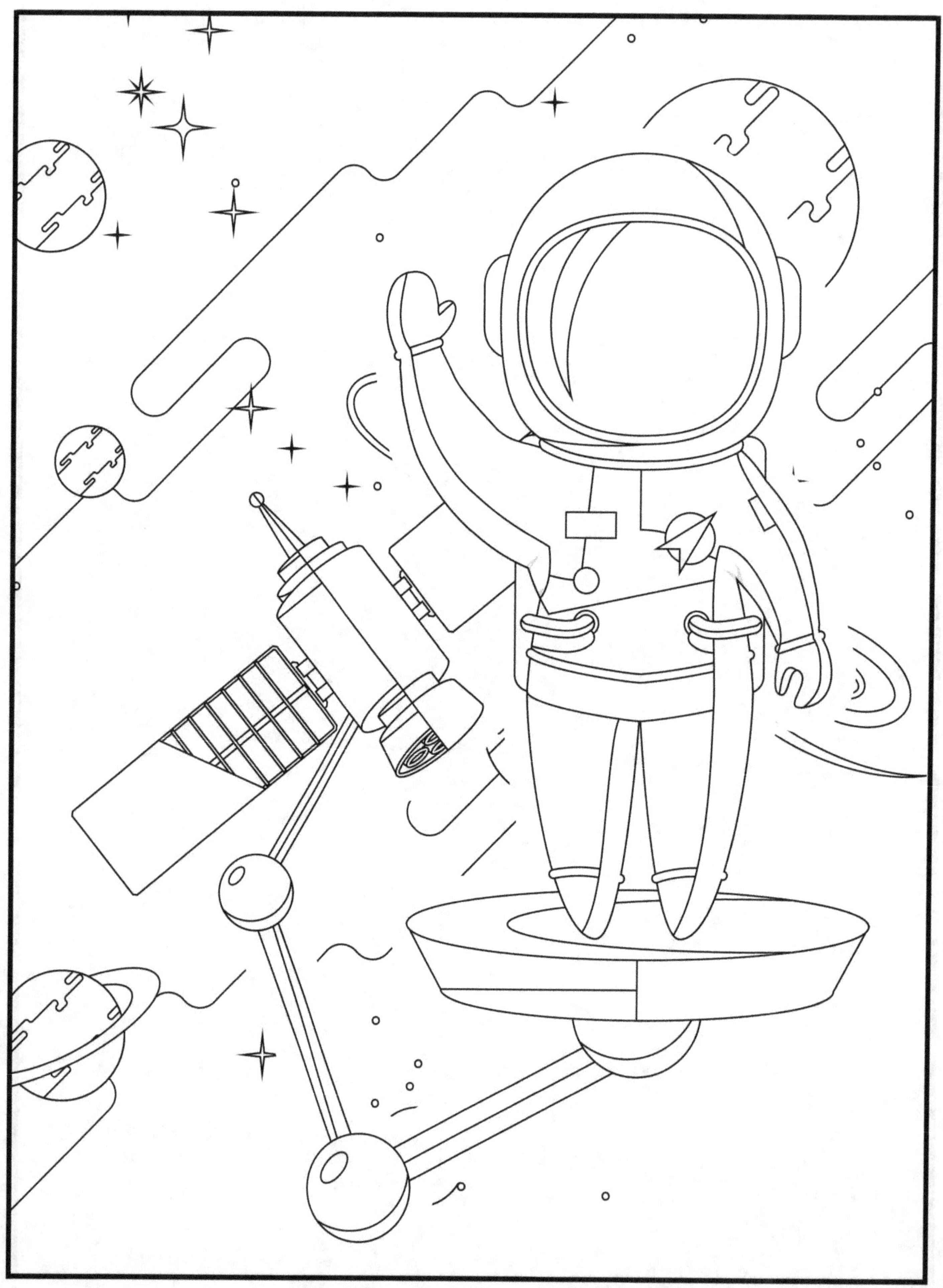

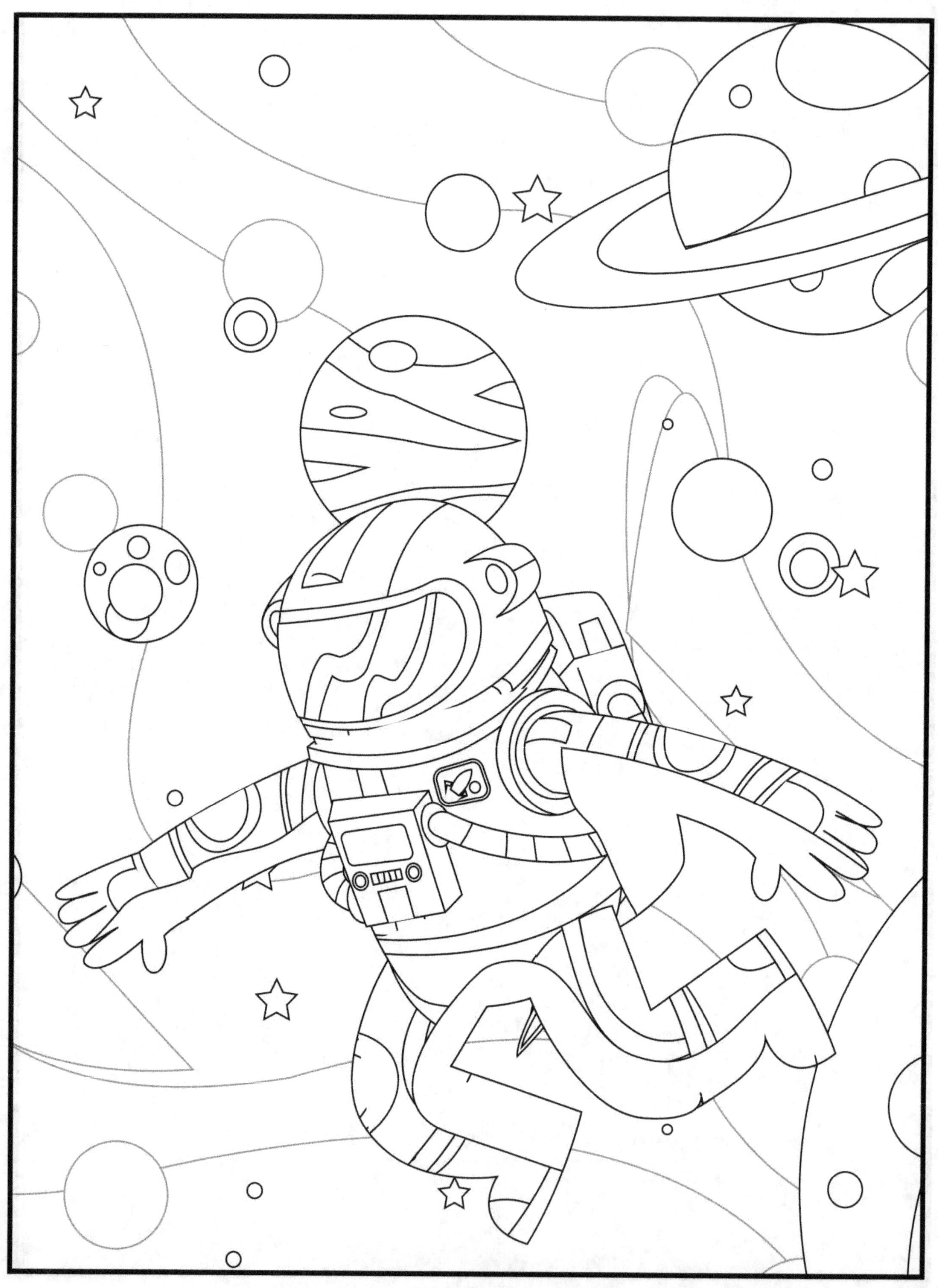

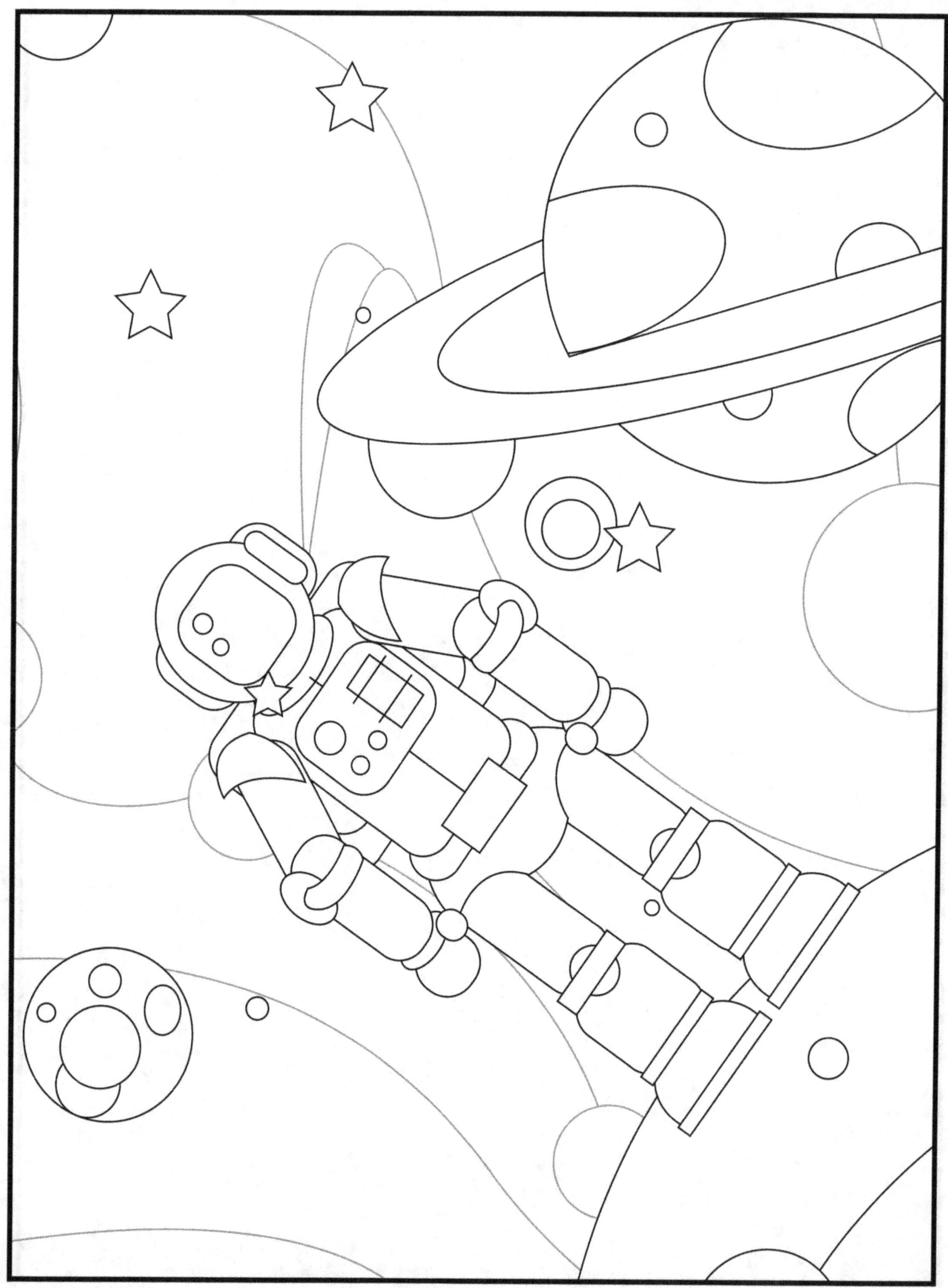

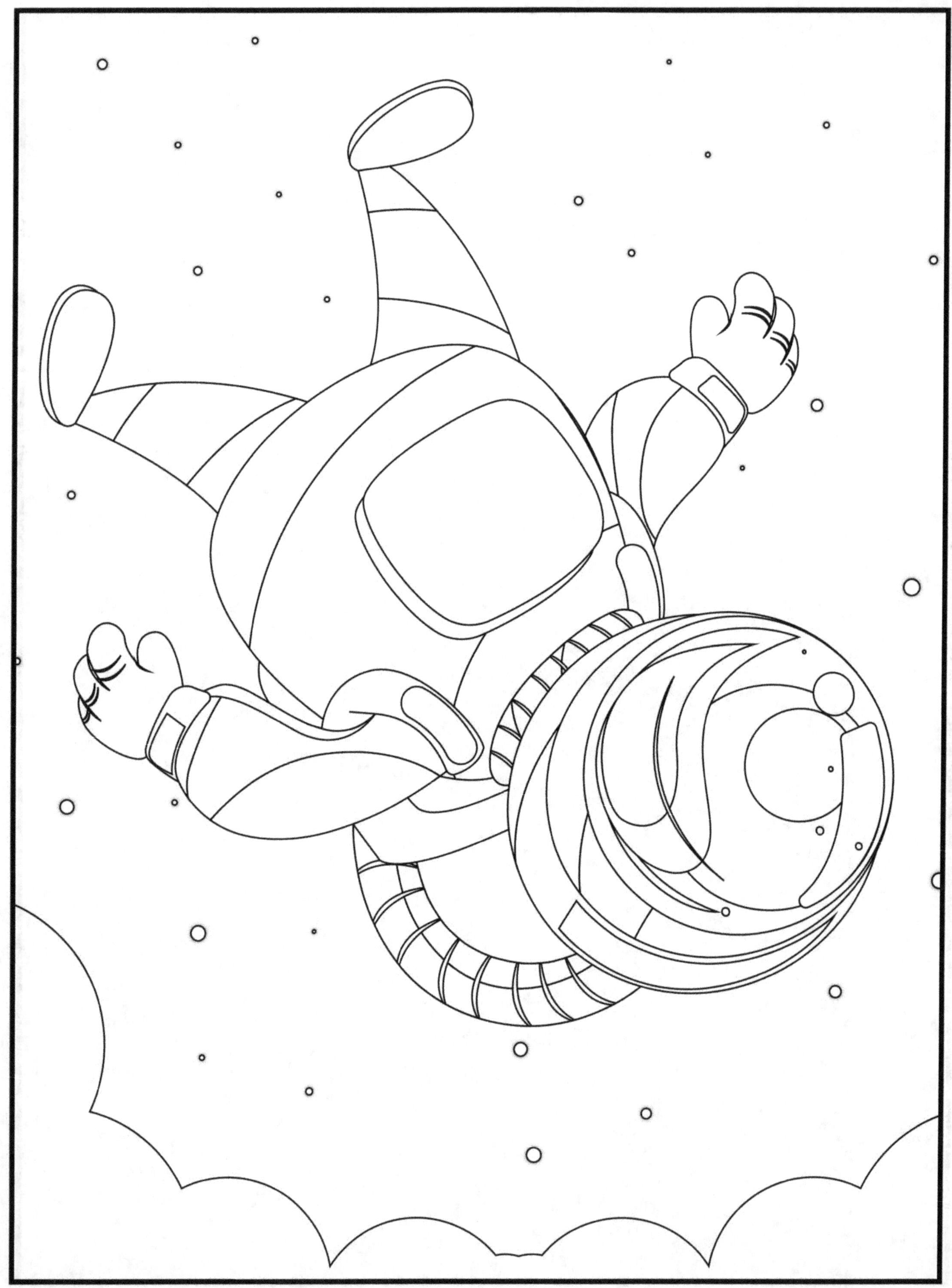

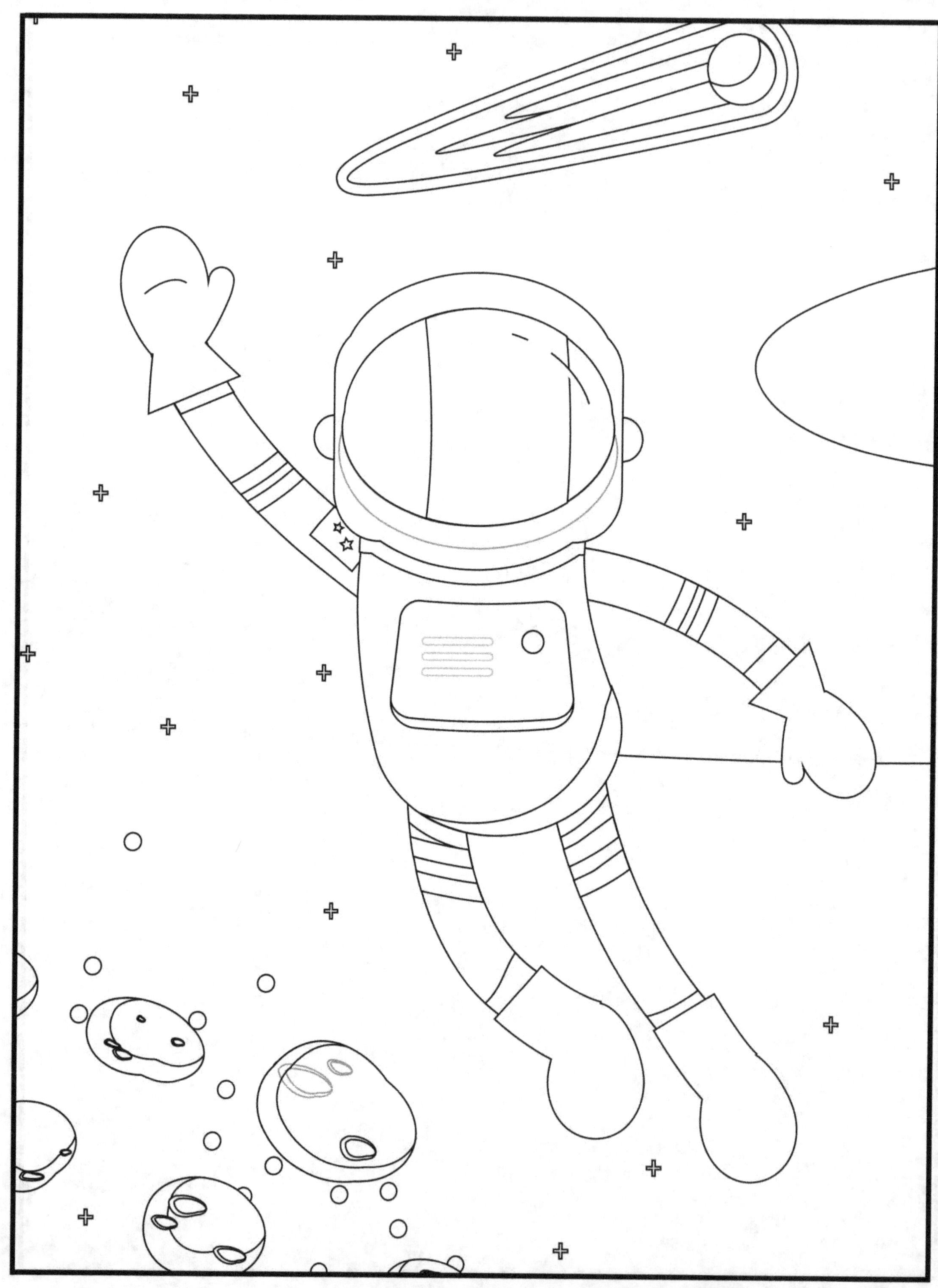

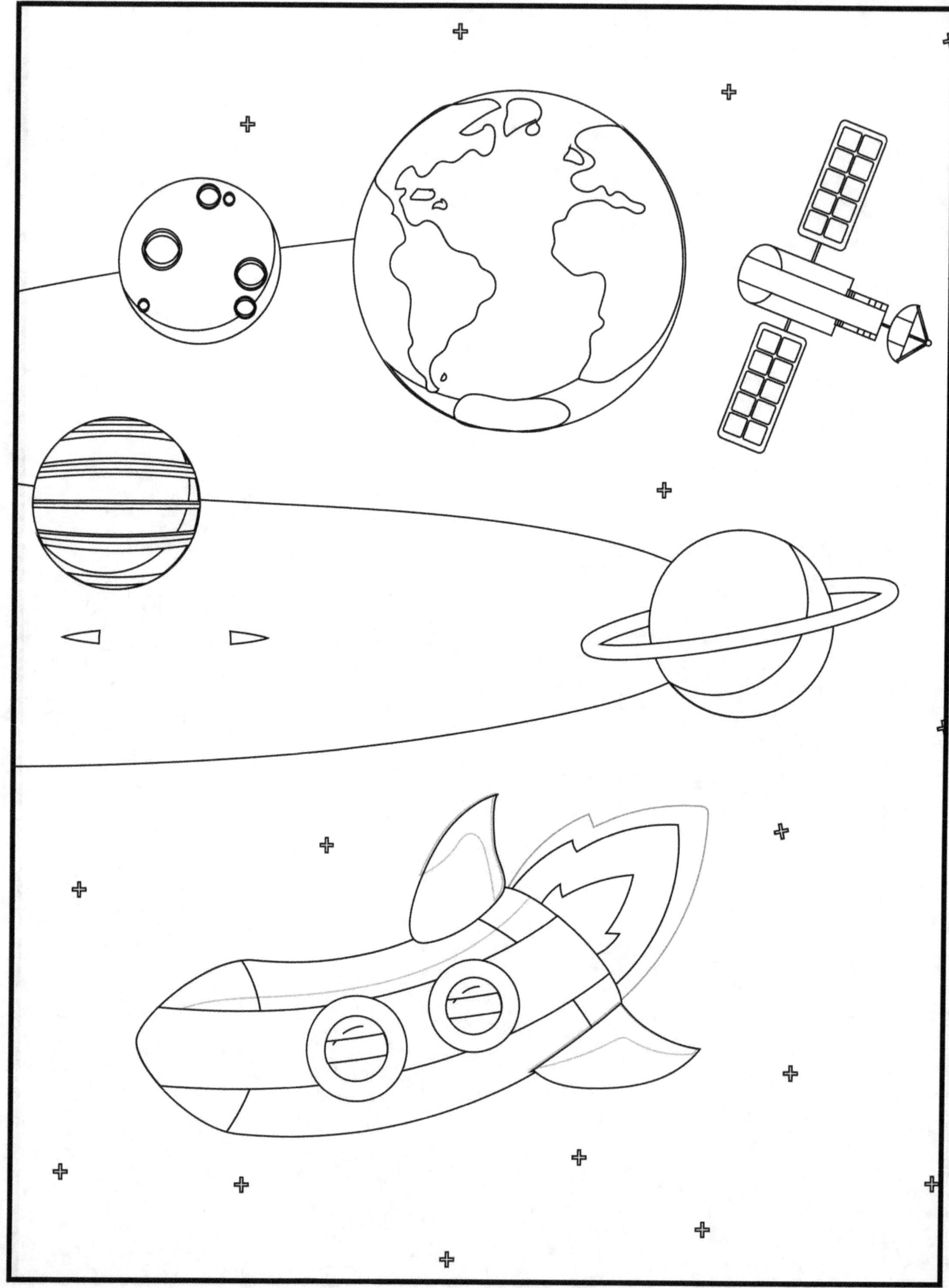

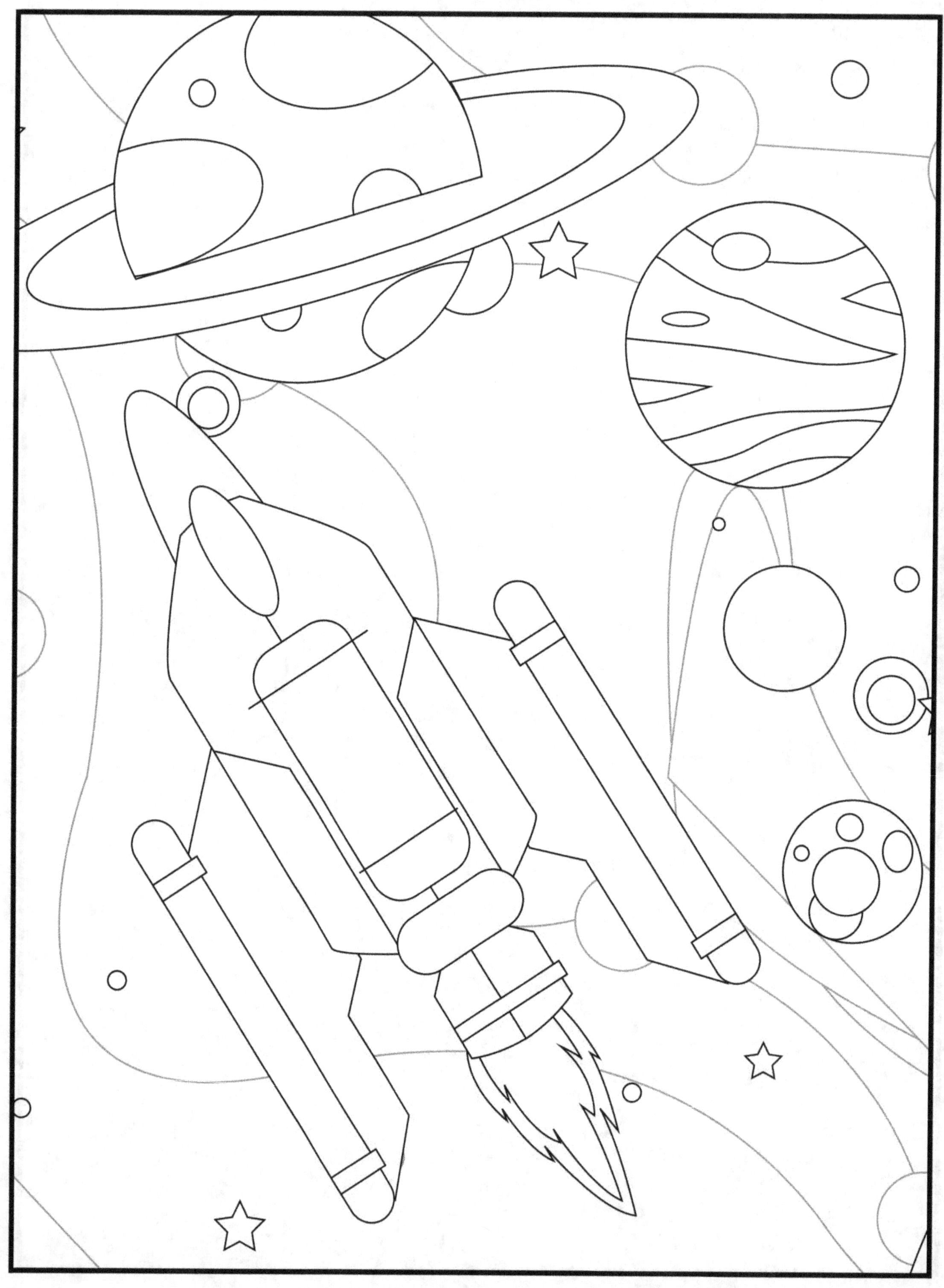

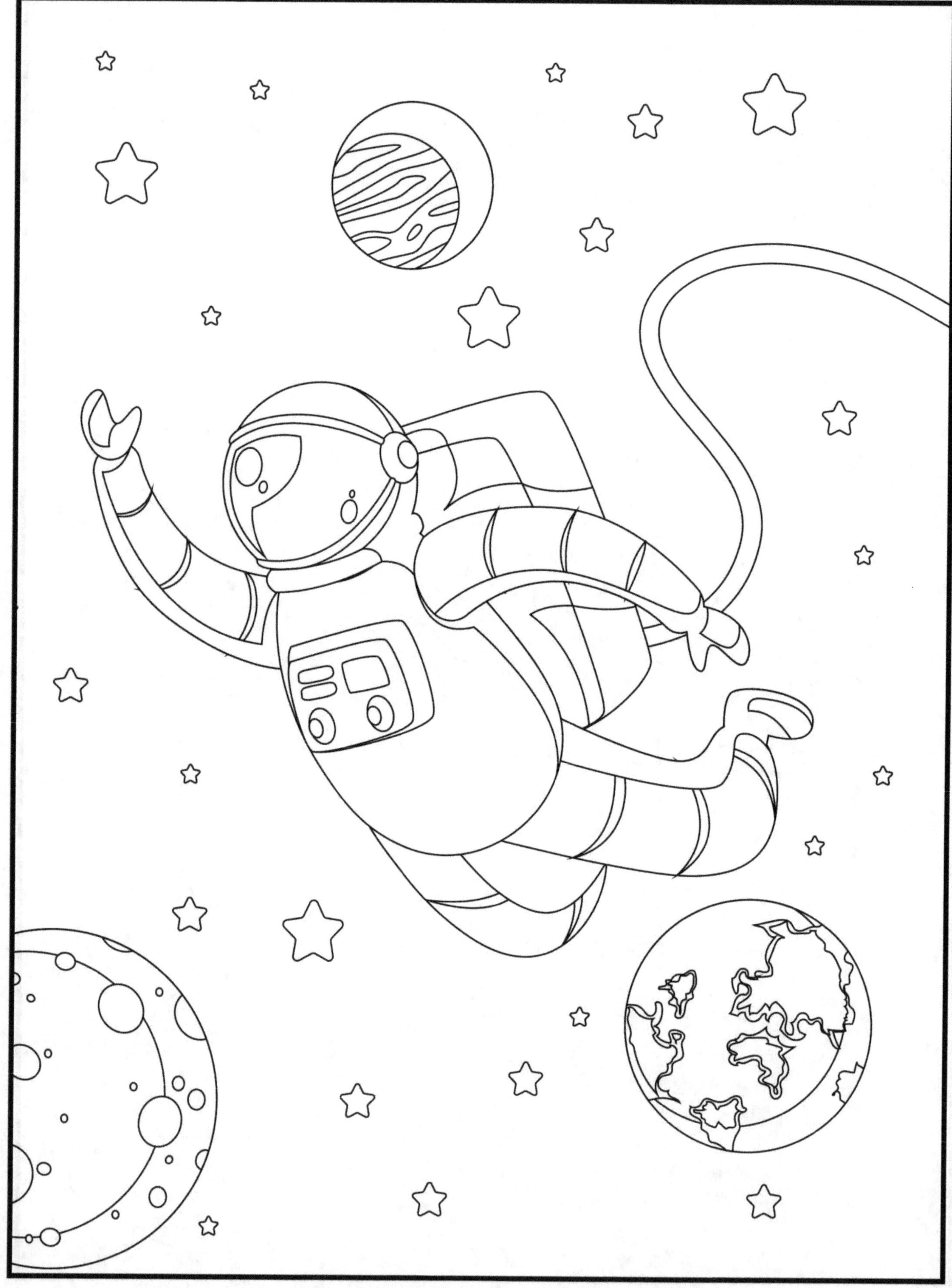

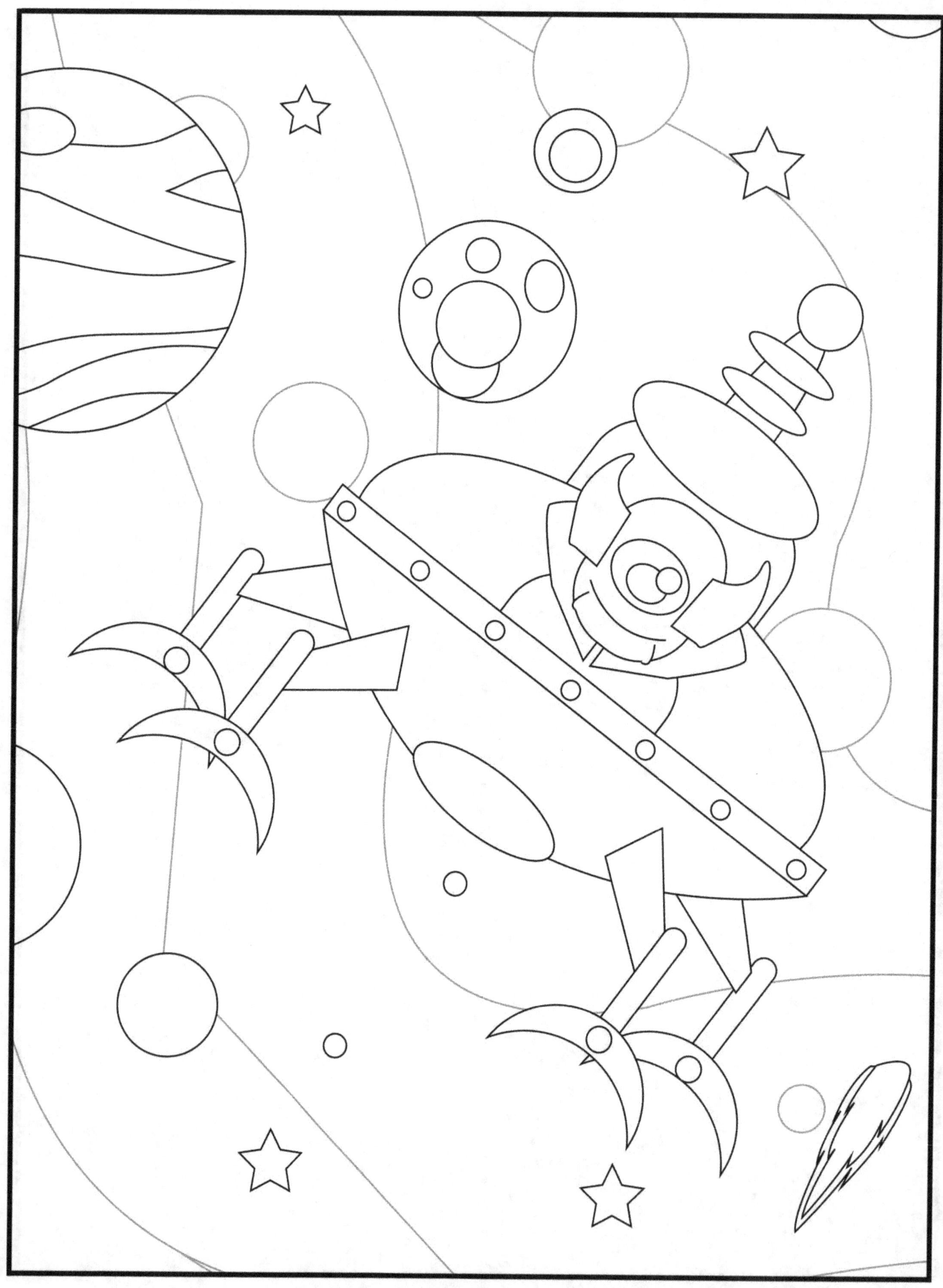

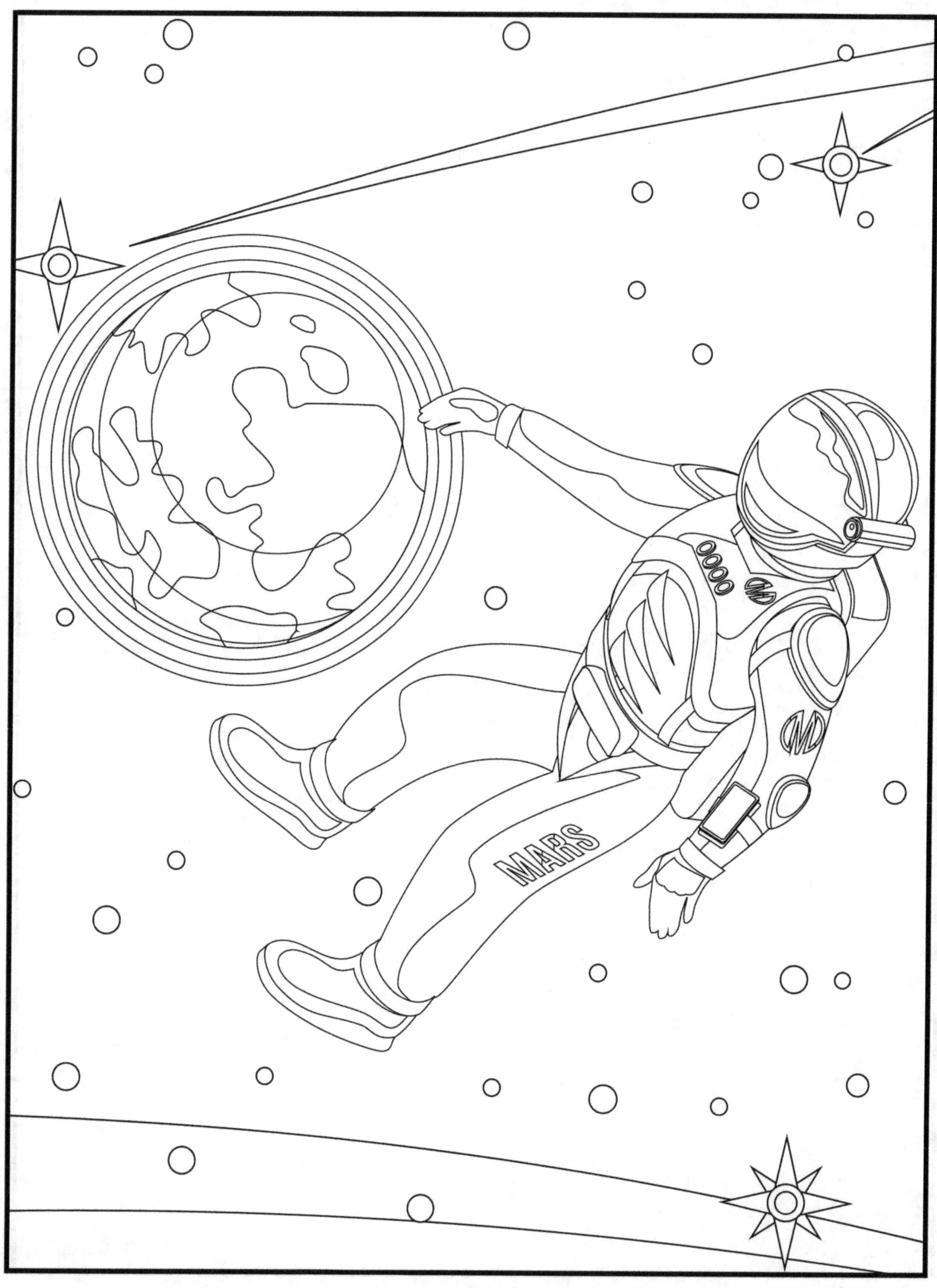

MARS

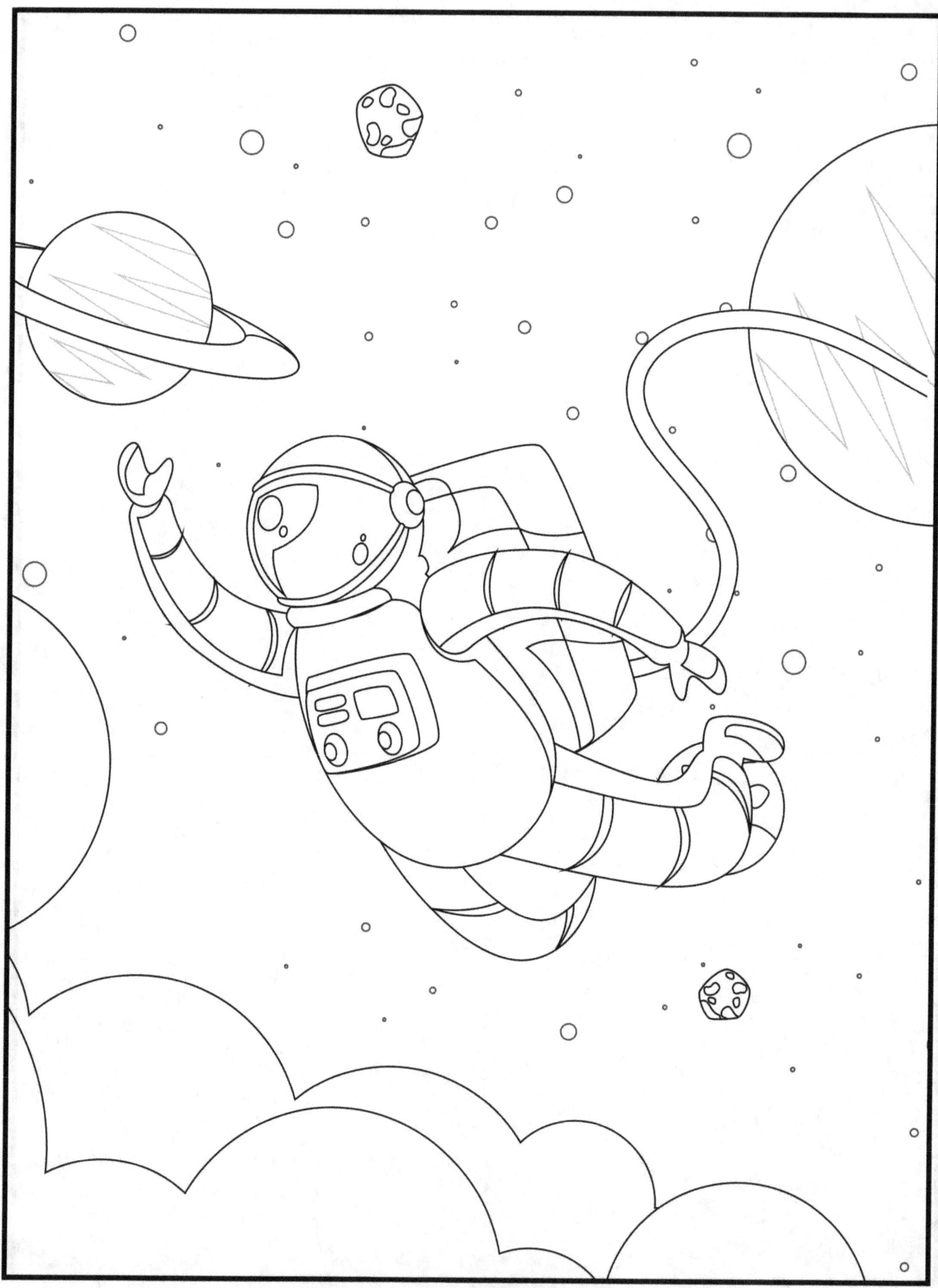

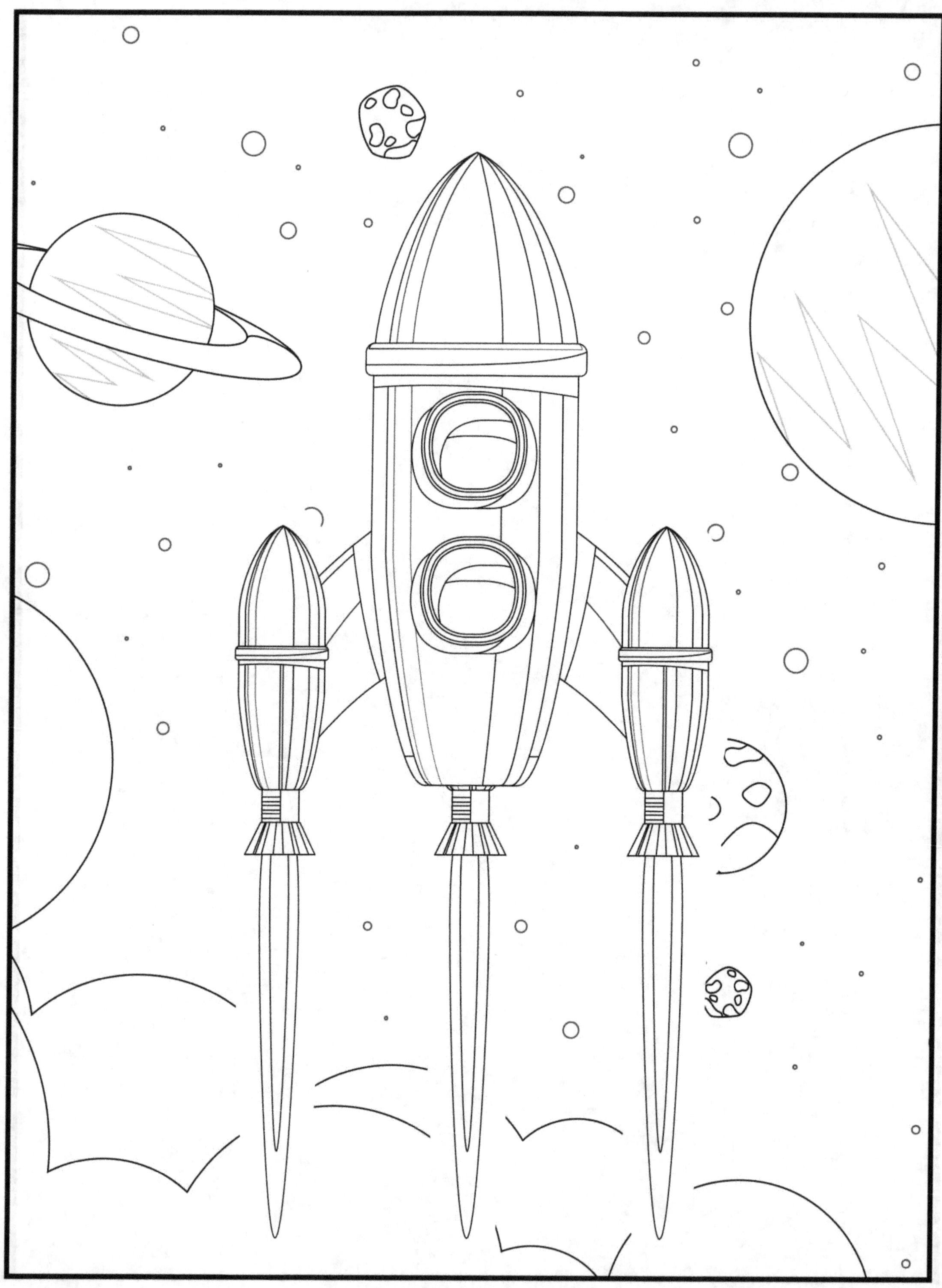

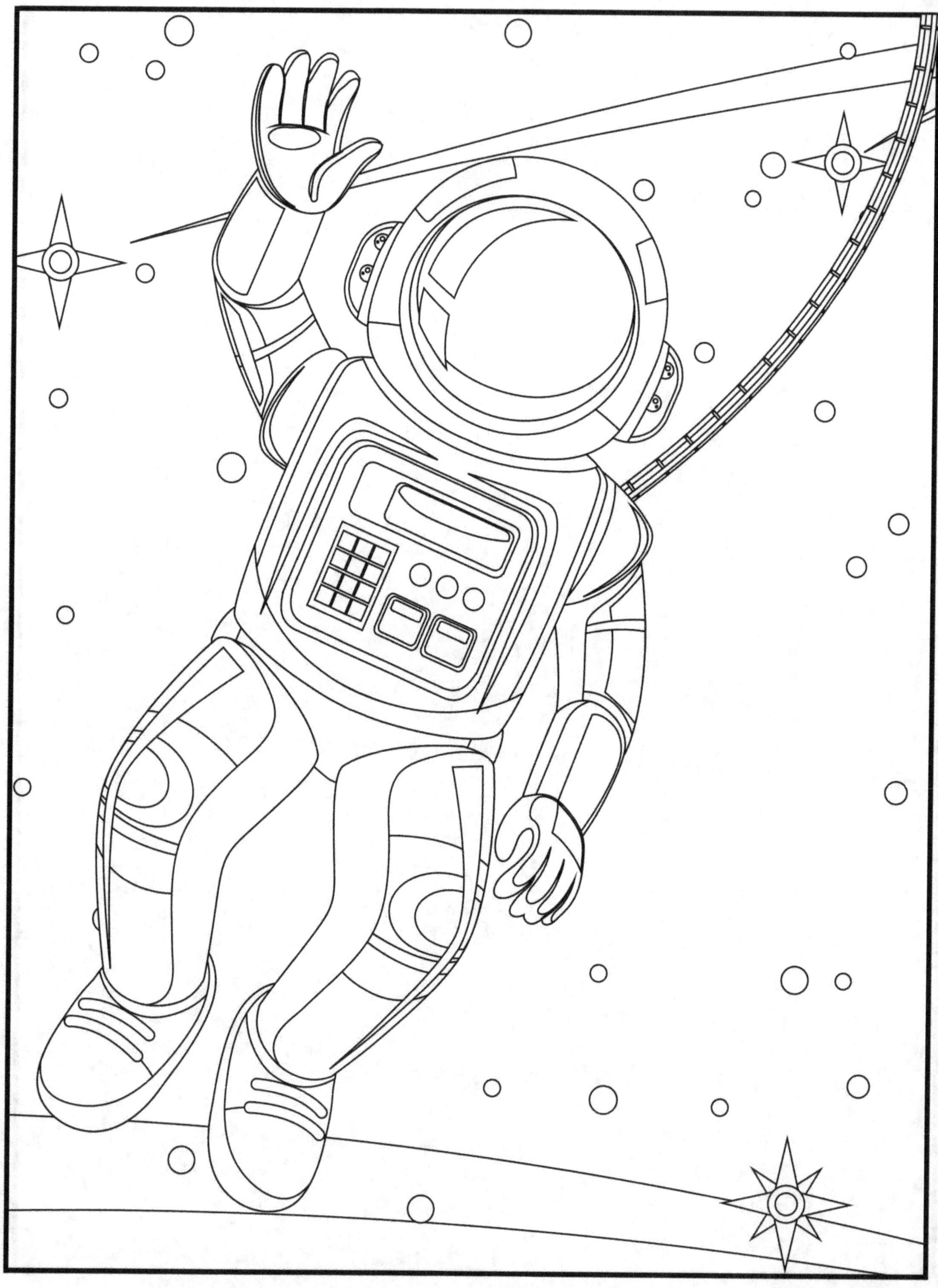

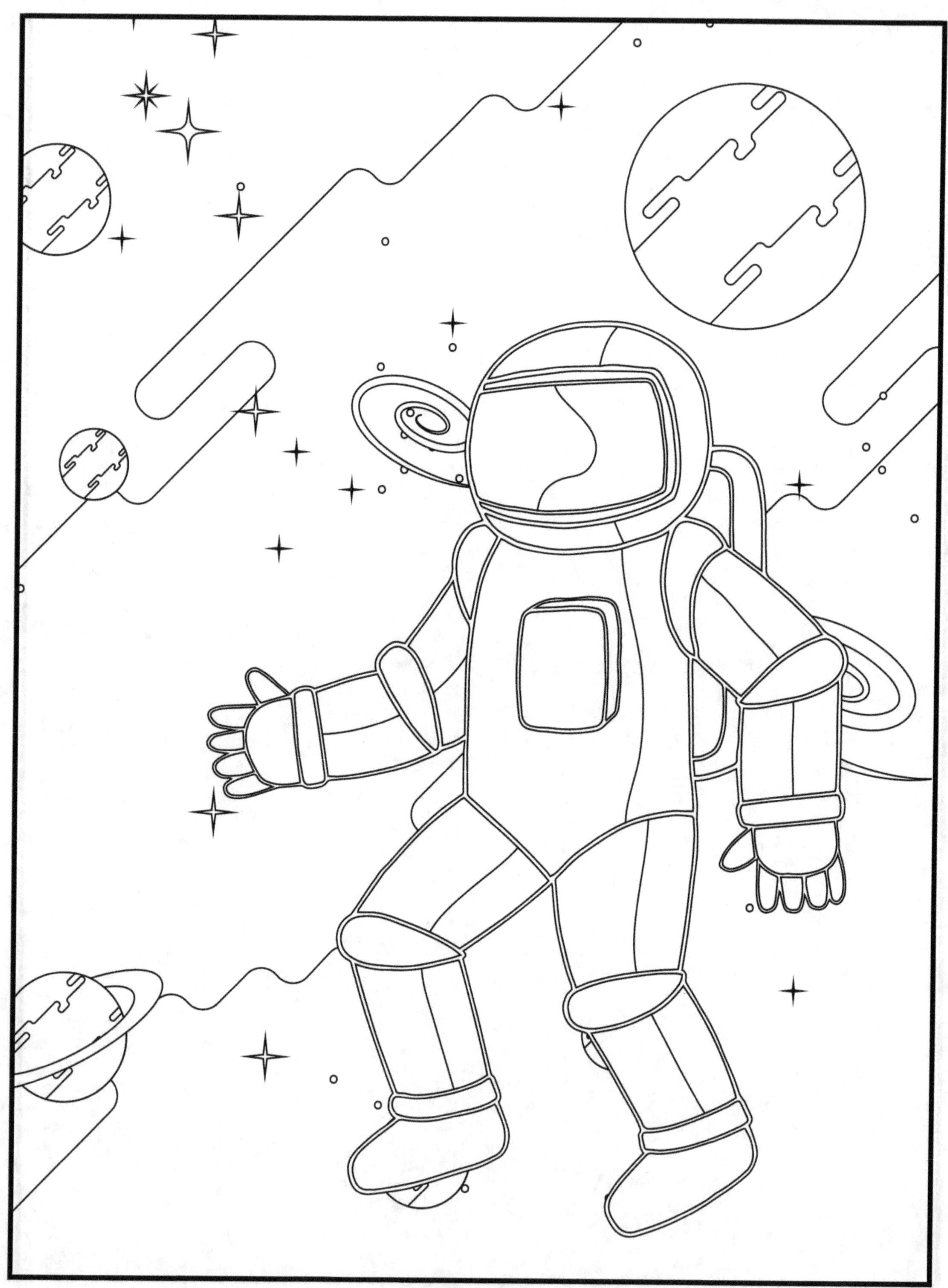

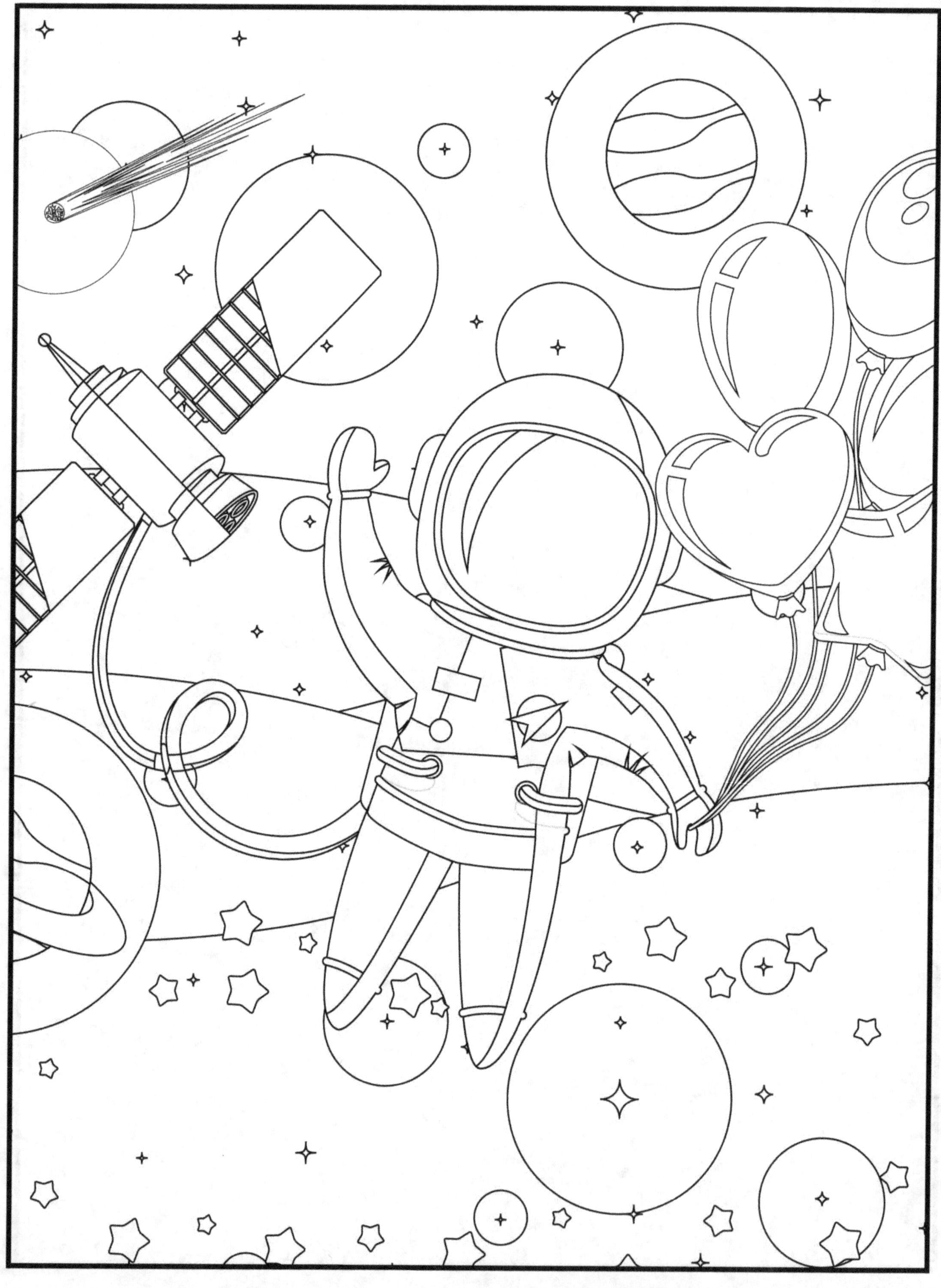

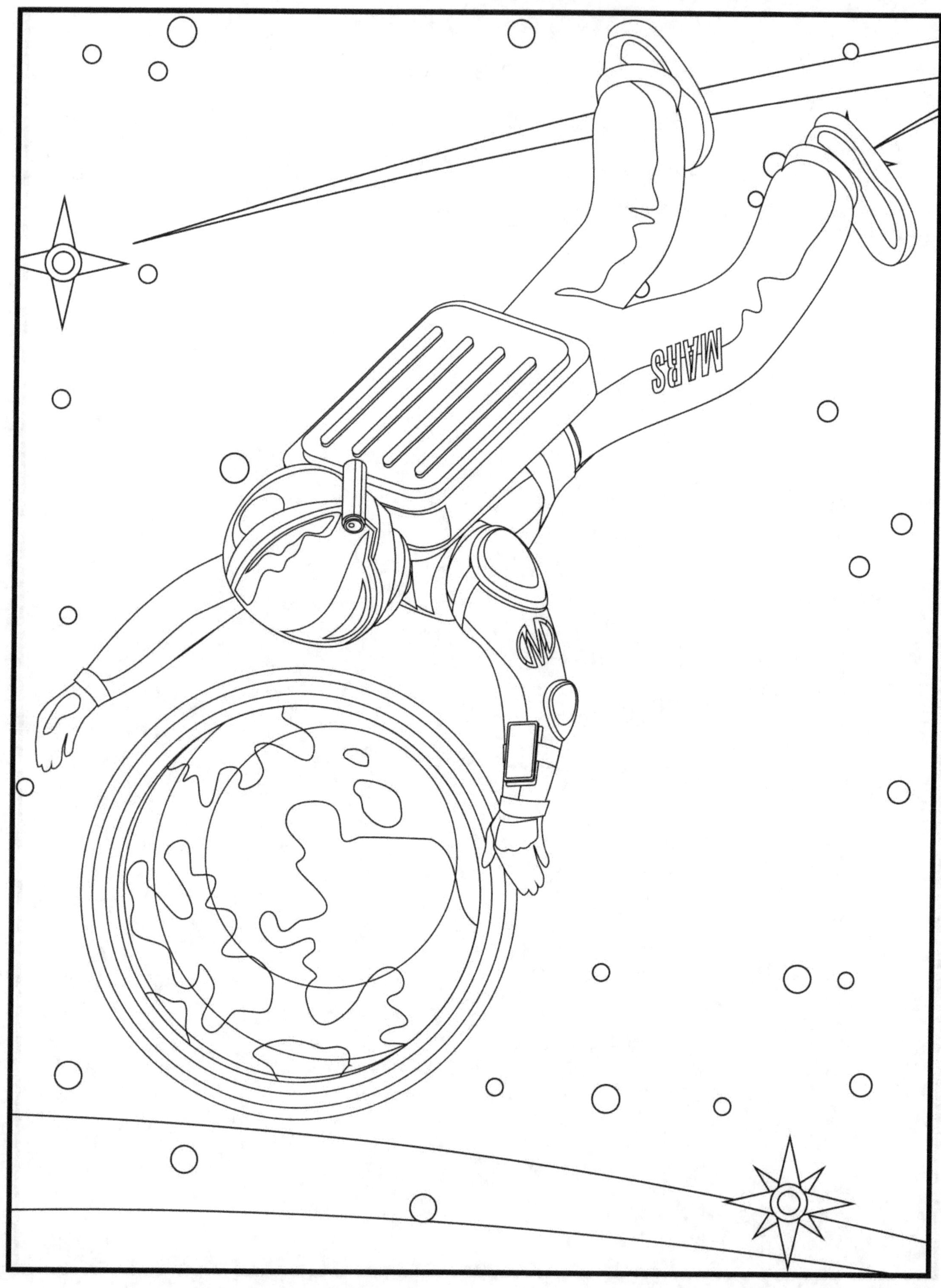

MARS

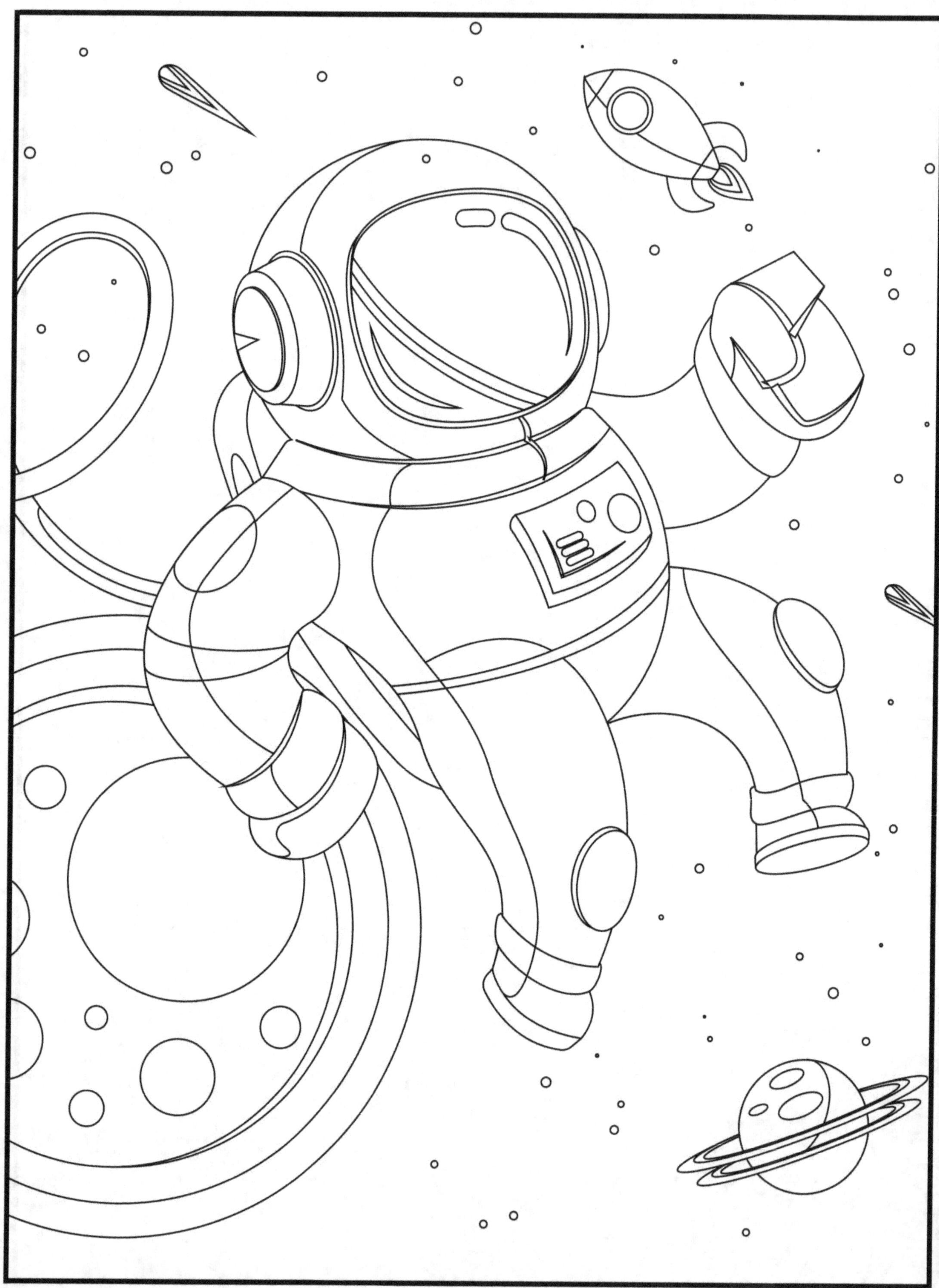

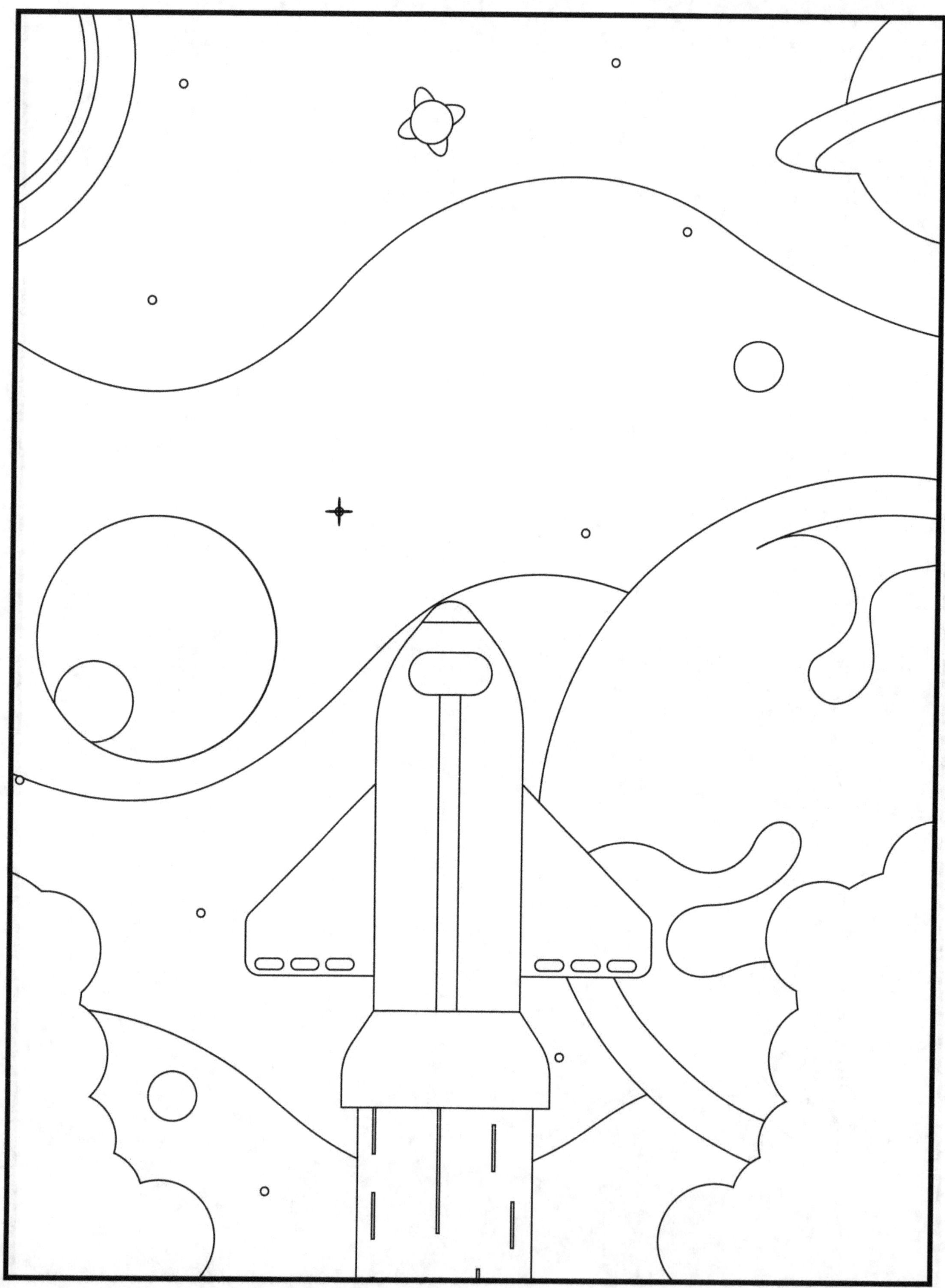

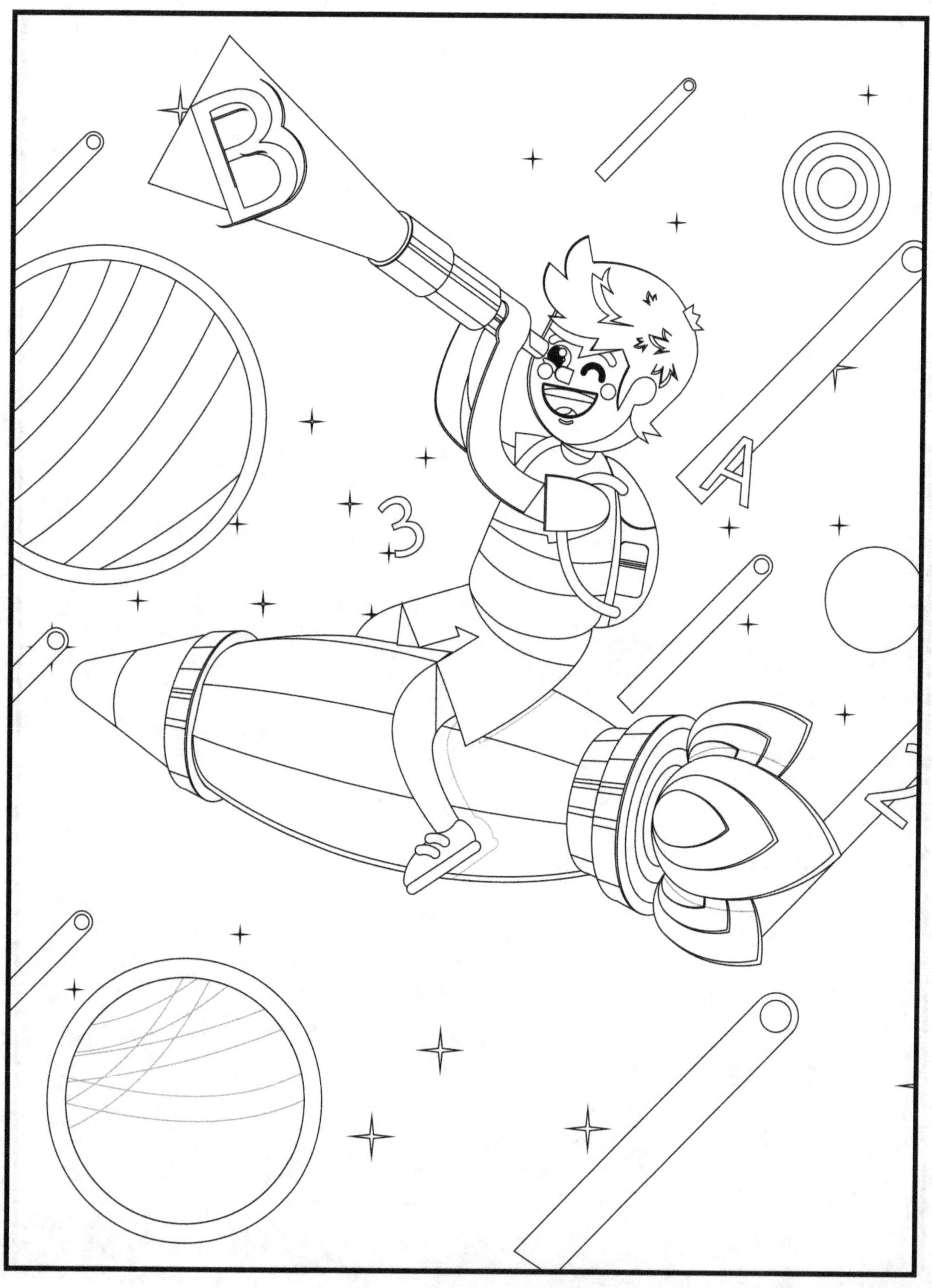

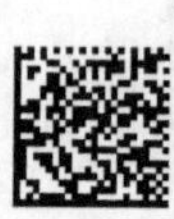
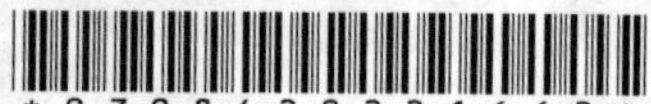